RIBBON B·A·S·I·C·S

Ribbon
B·A·S·I·C·S

All the Stitches & Techniques of
Silk Ribbon Work & Embroidery

Mary Jo Hiney & Joy Anckner

Sterling Publishing Co., Inc.   New York
A STERLING/CHAPELLE BOOK

For Chapelle Ltd.

Owner: Jo Packham
Editor: Cherie Hanson
Staff: Trice Boerens, Malissa Boatwright, Rebecca Christensen, Holly Fuller, Holly Hollingsworth, Susan Jorgenson, Susan Laws, Amanda McPeck, Jamie Pierce, Leslie Ridenour, Cindy Stoeckl, Nancy Whitley, and Lorrie Young
Photographer: Kevin Dilley for Hazen Photography

For Creative Beginnings

Owners: Erik, Debi, Jason, and Jim Linker
Staff: Mary Jo Hiney, Mona McKelvy, and Lisa Trett

Illustrations: Sally Vedder-Morley and Joy Anckner
Original artwork, techniques, and ribbon embroidery by Mary Jo Hiney
Original artwork and monogram concept by Joy Anckner

For information on where to purchase specialty items in this book please write to: Chapelle Ltd. Customer Service Department, P.O. Box 9252, Ogden, Ut 84409.

Library of Congress Cataloging-in-Publication Data

Hiney, Mary Jo.
    Ribbon basics : all the stitches & techniques of ribbon work & embroidery / Mary Jo Hiney, Joy Anckner.
        p. cm.
    "A Sterling/Chapelle book."
    Includes index.
    ISBN 0-8069-1294-4
    1. Silk ribbon embroidery. 2. Ribbon work. 3. Flowers in art.
I. Anckner, Joy. II. Title.
TT778.S64H56 1995
746.44—dc20
                                   94–45684
                                      CIP

A Sterling/Chapelle Book

1 3 5 7 9 10 8 6 4 2

First paperback edition published in 1995 by
Sterling Publishing Company, Inc.
387 Park Avenue South, New York, N.Y. 10016
Produced by Chapelle Ltd.
P.O. Box 9252, Newgate Station, Ogden, Utah 84409
© 1995 by Chapelle Ltd.
Distributed in Canada by Sterling Publishing
% Canadian Manda Group, One Atlantic Avenue, Suite 105
Toronto, Ontario, Canada M6K 3E7
Distributed in Great Britain and Europe by Cassell PLC
Wellington House, 125 Strand, London WC2R 0BB, England
Distributed in Australia by Capricorn Link (Australia) Pty Ltd.
P.O. Box 6651, Baulkham Hills, Business Centre, NSW 2153, Australia
Printed and Bound in U.S.A.

Sterling ISBN 0-8069-1294-4 Trade
0-8069-1295-2 Paper

Mary Jo Hiney

Mary Jo Hiney's ongoing love of ribbon embroidery and ribbon work are an extension of the needlework and sewing skills she learned from her mother. In this book, her skill and precision serve her well as she invents new stitches and techniques to share with you. Mary Jo emphasizes that there are no mistakes; only variations, and in those variations lie creativity.

Mary Jo attended the Los Angeles Fashion Institute of Design and Merchandising. She worked in the wardrobe department of NBC Studios in Burbank, California, where she dressed such stars as Lucille Ball and Maureen O'Hara.

Now Mary Jo works for Creative Beginnings, designing its silk ribbon embroidery kits. Working with silk ribbon, fine laces, trims and charms is a process Mary Jo relishes.

Many of her additional techniques and designs are exhibited in her book, *Victorian Ribbon & Lacecraft Designs,* also published by Sterling/Chapelle. It is Mary Jo's hope that these techniques will add beauty and dimension to your life.

Dedication

This book is dedicated to life's challenges; the ones that deepen our appreciation and increase our wisdom, so that we may live life more fully.

Joy Anckner

Joy Anckner lives at the base of the Wasatch Mountains in northern Utah with her husband and four sons. She was raised in central Kansas by talented and creative parents. Joy's talents as a craftsperson stem from learning to sew and embroider at a very young age under the tutelage of her grandmothers, mother and aunt. Also, a sense of heritage has been passed down to her with family heirlooms, including a piece of lace knitted by her great-great-great grand-mother while she was on a ship bound for America from Sweden.

Joy carries on the legacy with her own unique style. Her work reflects her love of antiques, Victorian "fancywork", and the study of herbs and flowers. Silk ribbon embroidery has provided the perfect opportunity for her to display her designing talents. She feels that silk ribbon works with such body and comes in so many brilliant, vibrant colors that its uses are limitless in needle-work.

Joy also enjoys playing and singing the blues, hand coloring her own black-and-white photography, gardening and animal husbandry.

Contents

General Ribbon Techniques

Tracing

When tracing designs onto fabric, use an erasable marking pen, but do not transfer all marks. Use pen as a general placement guide; too many pen marks become confusing.

Tips

Always keep the ribbon flat while working embroidery stitches. Untwist the ribbon during each stitch and use the needle to lift/straighten the ribbon. Wrap the ribbon very flatly over the needle, so that each stitch uses the full ribbon width. Pull the ribbon very gently to allow the stitches to lie softly on top of the fabric. Be creative with your stitching. Exact stitch placement is not critical, but you will want to make sure any placement marks are covered by silk ribbon stitches. Always keep in mind that there are no mistakes, there are only variations.

Needles

A size 3 crewel embroidery needle works well for most fabrics when using 4-mm silk ribbon. Purchase a mixed packet of crewel embroidery needles, sizes 1 to 5. As a rule of thumb, the barrel of the needle must create a hole large enough for the ribbon to pass through. The ribbon will hide the hole made by the needle. If the ribbon does not pull through the fabric easily enough, it is because a larger needle is needed. Also, the eye of the needle must be large enough for the ribbon to lay flat when threaded. For 7-mm silk ribbon, use a chenille needle, available in sizes 18 to 24.

To Thread Ribbon on the Needle

Thread the ribbon through the eye of the needle. With the tip of the needle, pierce the center of the ribbon ¼" from end. Pull remaining ribbon through to "lock" ribbon on the needle.

To Begin Stitching

There are two methods to begin stitching. The first is the "soft-knot" method and the second is the "stitch-through-tail" method. The "soft-knot" is to be used only for the first color of your embroidery. Begin by folding the end of the ribbon over on itself and pierce through the fold with the needle. Gently pull the ribbon through itself to leave a loop at the end. Insert the needle in the fabric and pull the ribbon very gently through the fabric, being careful not to pull the loop through the fabric.

Soft-Knot-Method

Use the "stitch-through-tail method for the rest of your colors. Bring the ribbon up through the fabric, leaving a ½" tail of ribbon hanging on the underside of the fabric. When you make your first stitch, pierce through the ribbon tail on the back side, at about ¼" from the ribbon end.

Stitch-Through-Method

To End Stitching

Bring the ribbon through to the underside of the fabric. Lay the ribbon across the nearest stitch and stitch through both the ribbon and the nearest stitch. Stitch through the ribbon and stitch again to lock the last stitch. Clip the ribbon near the knot and cut off the ribbon at the eye of the needle.

12

Letter

Twist a short length of striped ribbon. Pin to fabric at crossbar of "A". Slipstitch edges of coiled ribbon with invisible or matching thread. Twist another short length of striped ribbon. Pin to fabric to the left side of "A", allowing bottom edge to fold. Slipstitch and tuck edges of twisted ribbon to form letter. Repeat for the right side of the letter "A". The letter is formed by sculpting the ribbon and then tacking it to the fabric.

Anemone

1. Cut two 8½" lengths of ⅝" wired ivory ribbon for each anemone. Beginning and ending ¼" from ends, mark ribbon at 2" intervals, as shown in diagram.

2. GATHER-STITCH each length of ribbon, following blue stitching line; see diagram. Pull thread tightly to gather petals. Connect first and last petals, securing with stitches. Repeat with remaining length.

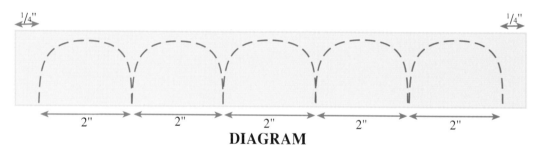

DIAGRAM

3. Place one layer of petals over the other to form the base for the anemone. Stitch each layer together in the middle of the flower to hold it in place. Make sure that the petals on the top layer are situated between the petals in the second layer.

4. Repeat Steps 1, 2, and 3 to make two anemones.

5. Using green 7-mm silk ribbon, stitch large and small RIBBON STITCHES, forming large and small anemone leaves.

6. Place the anemones onto the fabric. Attach the bottom layer to fabric with thread in centers and floss at outer edges of petals. Leave top layer free at petals. Sculpt the petals to desired shape.

7. Using pink 4-mm silk ribbon, stitch RIBBON STITCHES, forming centers of the anemones.

8. To form the fuzzy center of the anemone, cut a 1¹/₂" length of 1¹/₂" wired brown ribbon. Trim wired edges. Fold ribbon into quarters and cut a circle. Fringe the two opposite edges of the ribbon. Leave a narrow area in the center of circle to GATHER STITCH. Stitch fringed ribbon to center of anemone, forcing it through the center so that the fringe stands straight up. Once placed and stitched, trim fringe to desired length.

9. Using ivory 7-mm silk ribbon, stitch straight stitches, forming anemone buds. Stitch sepals on the buds with green 4-mm silk ribbon using the RIBBON STITCH.

Apple Blossoms, Branches, and Leaves

1. Handling six strands of brown embroidery floss as one, COUCH on fabric, forming branches; see photo. Weave a lighter shade of floss through the first.

2. Alternating white and two shades of pink 4-mm silk ribbon, stitch RIBBON STITCHES, forming apple blossoms. Some stitches can be PADDED with a second RIBBON STITCH to intensify the color and add dimension.

3. Stitch a PISTIL STITCH in the center of ribbon stitches, with one strand of brown embroidery floss.

4. Using green 4-mm silk ribbon, stitch LAZY DAISY STITCHES, forming leaves.

Asters, Aster Stems, and Leaves

1. For each aster, use three to four complementary shades of 4-mm silk ribbon. Begin each full aster with a basic five-spoked shape; see diagram.

2. Add a second layer of RIBBON STITCHES on top of and between the first to add shape and dimension; see diagram.

3. Stitch the center of each aster with one or two LOOPED RIBBON STITCHES.

4. Stitch STEM STITCHES with three strands of embroidery floss .

5. Using two shades of green 4-mm silk ribbon, stitch BULLIONED LAZY DAISY STITCHES, forming leaves.

DIAGRAM

Azalea and Leaves

1. Cut one 11" length and one 8" length of 1" ombré purple wired ribbon. Remove wire from darker edge. Beginning and ending $1/4$" from ends, mark 11" length of ribbon at $3^1/_2$" intervals, as shown in diagram.

2. GATHER-STITCH each length of ribbon, following blue stitching line, making SQUARED-OFF PETALS; see diagram. Pull thread tightly to gather petals. Connect first and last petals, securing with stitches. Repeat with 8" length, marking at $3^1/_2$" intervals.

3. Stitch three-petaled flower to fabric where indicated in pattern. Tack center edge of each petal $1/4$" in so that it appears ruffled. Stitch two-petaled flower on top of three-petaled flower. Using yellow 4-mm silk ribbon, PISTIL-STITCH in the center of azalea.

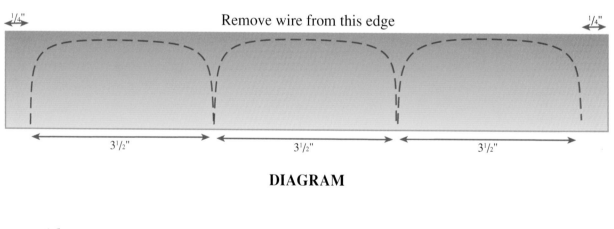

Remove wire from this edge

$1/4$" $1/4$"

$3^1/_2$" $3^1/_2$" $3^1/_2$"

DIAGRAM

Alyssums

Stitch loosely wrapped FRENCH KNOTS, randomly alternating four different shades of purple 4-mm silk ribbon to form alyssums. To add dimension, stitch green seed beads in each cluster of alyssums.

Glue charms as desired.

Astrautia Flowers

1. Using light brown 4-mm silk ribbon, stitch long LAZY DAISY STITCHES, forming the flower's basic shape; see diagram.

2. Using light pink 4-mm silk ribbon, stitch a RIBBON STITCH down center of each LAZY DAISY STITCH; see diagram.

3. Using coral 4-mm silk ribbon, shade each LAZY DAISY STITCH with ONE-TWIST RIBBON STITCHES; see diagram.

| Step 1 | Step 2 | Step 3 |

DIAGRAM

4. COUCH six strands of green embroidery floss to fabric, forming stems.

5. Stitch FRENCH KNOTS in two of the flowers. Using green 7-mm silk ribbon, stitch ONE-TWIST RIBBON STITCHES, forming large leaves.

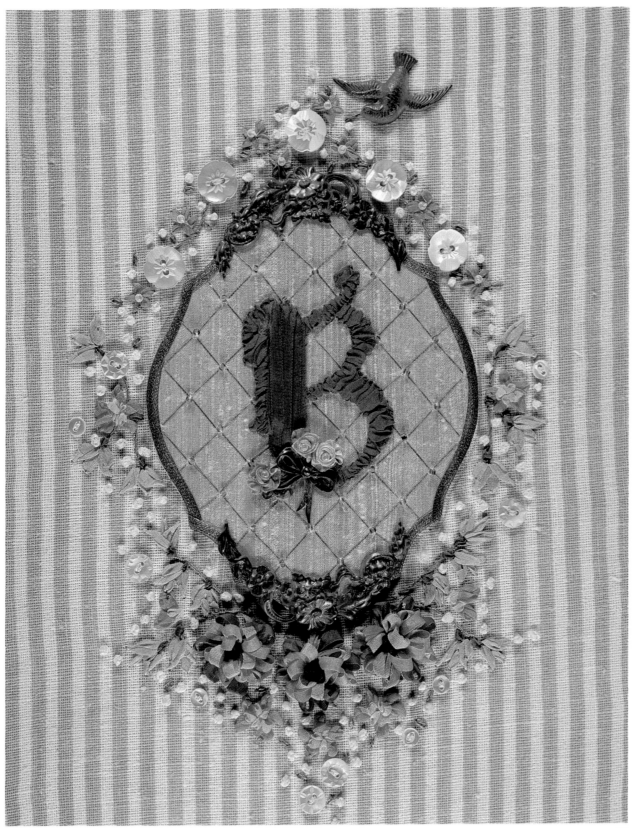

B

Letter

1. Make crest pattern. Cut one crest each from cardboard and fleece. Cut one crest from fabric, adding $\frac{1}{2}$" to all edges. Center and trace the letter "B" onto the fabric. Glue fleece to cardboard. Wrap and glue fabric around fleece/cardboard crest.

2. To make cross-hatching, use two strands of metallic embroidery floss. Stitch long STRAIGHT STITCHES, alternating with tiny stitches at each cross point on the fabric.

3. With 4-mm silk ribbon, embroider the letter "B" with RIBBON STITCHES, SATIN-STITCH STYLE. Sew one seed bead at each cross point. Hot-glue braid to outside edge of crest.

4. Trace the outline of the crest onto fabric with erasable marking pen. The outline is for placement only. Do not attach the crest to the fabric until all embroidery is completed.

5. After all flowers are stitched, stitch LAZY DAISY STITCHES with two strands of green embroidery floss, forming leaves. Stitch pearl buttons as desired. Glue the crest in place. Embellish the letter "B" with three ROSETTES made from three shades of blue 4-mm silk ribbon. Place a tiny pearl in center of each rosette. Place charms as desired.

Bachelor Buttons

1. Using a dark shade of 4-mm silk ribbon, stitch seven CROSSOVER LOOP STITCHES at the outside of the circle, forming Layer 1; see diagram.

2. Using a medium shade of 4-mm silk ribbon, stitch seven CROSSOVER LOOP STITCHES between Layer 1 loops and closer to center of circle, forming Layer 2; see diagram.

3. Using a light shade of 4-mm silk ribbon, stitch seven CROSSOVER LOOP STITCHES between Layer 2 loops and closest to center of circle; see diagram.

4. Using the darker shade of 4-mm silk ribbon, stitch three LOOPED RIBBON STITCHES at center of circle; see diagram. Fill in any spaces with RIBBON STITCHES.

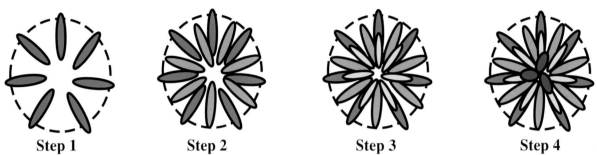

Step 1   Step 2   Step 3   Step 4

DIAGRAM

Buttercup Flowers

1. Using one shade of yellow 4-mm silk ribbon, stitch five CRISS-CROSSED LAZY DAISY STITCHES, forming Layer 1; see diagram.

2. Using a second shade of yellow 4-mm silk ribbon, stitch five LOOPED RIBBON STITCHES between each CRISSCROSSED LAZY DAISY STITCH, forming Layer 2; see diagram.

Step 1   Step 2

DIAGRAM

Bell Flowers

1. Using silk embroidery floss, stitch STEM STITCHES, forming bell flower stems.

2. Using blue 4-mm silk ribbon, stitch RIBBON STITCHES, forming the center petal; see diagram. For the outside petals, stitch two BULLIONED LAZY DAISY STITCHES, facing the petals outward from each other; see diagram.

3. For the bell flower leaves, stitch tiny RIBBON STITCHES with green 4-mm silk ribbon; see diagram.

Step 2-A   **Step 2-B**   **Step 3**
                    DIAGRAM

Baby Blue Eyes

1. Following the photograph for placement, stitch stems with silk embroidery floss.

2. Using blue 4-mm silk ribbon, stitch five RIBBON STITCHES in a spoke shape; see diagram. Stitch a 2¹/₂-mm pearl in the center of each flower; see diagram.

DIAGRAM

Baby's Breath

Using white 4-mm silk ribbon, randomly stitch FRENCH KNOTS, using two tight wraps for each knot.

Bullion Lazy Daisy

1. Bring needle up through fabric at A. Insert needle back into fabric about ¹/₄" from A. Keeping ribbon flat, wrap ribbon one to two times around the tip of the needle. Hold the wraps down with thumb while pulling the needle through the fabric.

2. Insert the needle into fabric near the tip of the bullion. This stitch can be pointed in any direction, depending on where you insert the needle to complete the bullion.

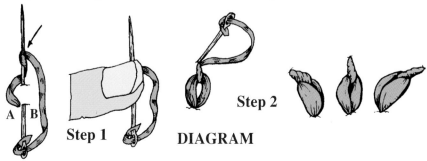

A B   **Step 1**   **Step 2**
                    DIAGRAM

Bullion Stitch

Bring the needle up through the fabric at A, then down through the fabric at B. Bring the needle up through the fabric again at A. Flatly wrap the ribbon around the needle three to four times. While holding your thumb on the wraps, pull the ribbon through the wrapped ribbon. Continue to pull the ribbon through until only the wraps remain on the surface of the fabric. Make and anchor stitch at B to end the stitch.

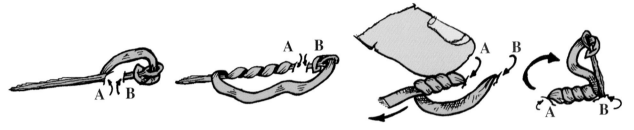

DIAGRAM

Backstitch

Bring the needle up through the fabric at A, then down through the fabric at B. Bring the needle up through the fabric again at C.

DIAGRAM

Buttonhole Stitch

Buttonhole stitches create a distinct pattern and are especially effective on edges. There, they serve as a tool for outlining as well. Bring needle up through fabric at A, then down through fabric at B. Bring needle up through fabric at C, then down through fabric at B. Bring needle up at D, then down again at E. Continue in this manner until desired length is achieved.

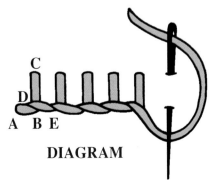

DIAGRAM

C

Letter

1. Trace design onto fabric with erasable marking pen. Place metallic braid on fabric, forming the letter "C". COUCH strands with invisible thread to secure.

2. Place ³/₁₆" green velvet ribbon in a diamond shape at center of fabric; tack with invisible thread to secure. Using two strands of gold metallic floss, zigzag-stitch over velvet ribbon for a decorative texture.

3. Place ³/₁₆" burgundy velvet ribbon to outer edge of design to frame; tack with invisible thread to secure. Place burgundy picot trim to inner borders of design; tack with invisible thread to secure.

Couching

Lay ribbon in place on fabric. Secure the ribbon by stitching thread or specified fiber around it; see diagram.

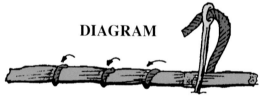

DIAGRAM

Crossover Looped Stitch

Bring ribbon up through fabric. Form a loop by overlapping the ribbon as in diagram. Pierce the ribbon with the needle; then take the ribbon down through the fabric.

DIAGRAM

Crisscrossed Lazy Daisy Stitch

Bring needle up through fabric at A. Crossover the first leg of the loop and insert the needle back into fabric right next to A, bringing it out again about 1/4" from A. Slip the ribbon under the tip of the needle and turn the edge of the ribbon so that it lays on its side. Hold loop down with thumb, while pulling ribbon through. Insert the needle back into fabric at top of loop and tack down.

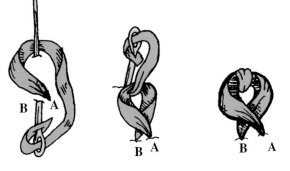

DIAGRAM

Clocks Vine

1. Place six strands of embroidery floss around fabric, forming vines; COUCH with another shade of floss to secure.

2. With green 1/4" satin ribbon, stitch leaves around vines, using the RIBBON STITCH. (Note: Use a large-pointed needle.)

3. Using orange 4-mm silk ribbon, stitch two RIBBON STITCHES and three CRISSCROSSED LAZY DAISY STITCHES; see diagram.

DIAGRAM

4. Using green 4-mm silk ribbon, stitch one LOOPED RIBBON STITCH, forming center of flower.

5. Using bronze 4-mm silk ribbon, stitch one BULLION LAZY DAISY STITCH, forming leaf.

Carnation

1. Place thin green rattail on fabric, forming stems. COUCH with floss to secure.

2. For each carnation, stitch short ends of a 12" length of $1/2$" satin iridescent ribbon together, forming a tube. Stitch a GATHERING STITCH on one edge of tube. Pull tightly to gather, forming a circular ruffle; secure thread.

3. Repeat to make three carnations. Stitch each flower to stem so that the flower lays open. Tack edges to create different effects as desired.

4. Using green $1/4$" satin ribbon, stitch a large RIBBON STITCH for calyx.

5. Using two shades of green 4-mm silk ribbon, stitch long ONE TWIST RIBBON STITCHES, forming leaves.

Chrysanthemum

1. Place green cording on fabric, forming stems. COUCH with floss to secure.

2. Cut fifteen 3" lengths of three shades of rose 4-mm silk ribbon. (For smaller mum, use ten 3" lengths.) Tie a knot in center of each length. Fold knotted length in half. Place lengths side by side and stitch a GATHERING STITCH with a $5/8$" seam; see diagram. Pull tightly to gather. Join the first and last lengths. Trim seam to $1/8$". Hand-sew to stem.

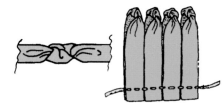

DIAGRAM

Spider Mum

See Spider Mum on page 122.

Coleus Leaves

Cut a 5" length of $^5/_8$" wired ribbon. Fold ribbon in half, matching short ends. Turn folded ribbon corners up $^1/_8$" from top edge. Following dashed line, stitch with GATHERING STITCHES; see diagram. Pull thread so that ribbon measures $1^1/_2$" long. Secure thread. Open and shape leaf. Tack leaf to fabric, hiding raw edge.

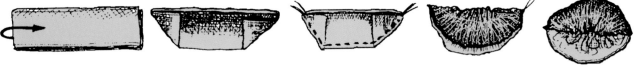

DIAGRAM

Cockscomb

1. Tie two shades of $^3/_{16}$" velvet ribbon into twelve knots each. Trim each knot so that $^1/_8$" of ribbon remains on each side of knot. Stitch knots bunched together on fabric, alternating colors and hiding raw edges under other knots.

2. Using two shades of green 7-mm silk ribbon, stitch RIBBON STITCHES next to knotted ribbon bunches for leaves.

Cascade

At a distance of $^1/_2$" from bow's knot, make a stitch about $^1/_8$" long. Now make a $^1/_8$"-long BACKSTITCH directly next to the first stitch. Repeat as above for next stitch. Allow the ribbon to curl and twist naturally. Continue to randomly stitch the ribbon to create desired effect. Repeat with remaining tail of bow.

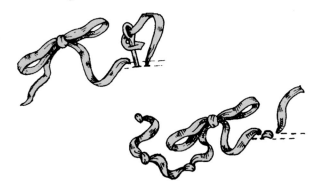

Delphinium

1. Cut an 8¹/₂" length each of ⁵/₈" ivory wired ribbon and ⁵/₈" sheer ribbon. Beginning and ending ¹/₄" from ends, mark each ribbon length at 2" intervals; see diagram. Stitch a GATHERING STITCH following blue stitching line. Pull thread tightly to gather petals. Connect the first and last petals; secure with stitches. Repeat with remaining ribbon length. Stitch the sheer petals on top of the wired petals.

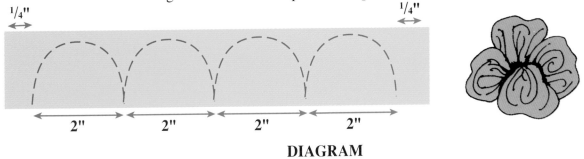

| ¹/₄" | | | | | ¹/₄" |

2"   **2"**   **2"**   **2"**

DIAGRAM

2. Repeat to make five delphiniums. Make buds as above, except use 4¹/₂" lengths of sheer ribbon. Make four buds.

3. Sew or glue three short strands of gold cord in center for stamens.

Daisy (English)

1. Cut twenty-one 2¹/₂" lengths of light pink ¹/₄" satin ribbon. Fold each length as in diagram. Stitch lengths together with a ⁵/₈" seam allowance, using the GATHERING STITCH. Pull thread tightly to gather petals. Trim seam allowance to ¹/₄". Stitch petals to fabric where indicated.

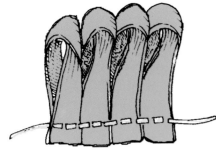

DIAGRAM

2. Using pink 4-mm silk ribbon, stitch LONG RIBBON STITCHES within most of the gathered petals to anchor them, yet allowing some to float freely.

3. Using bright pink 4-mm silk ribbon, stitch SATIN-STYLE RIBBON STITCHES, forming the centers of the daisies. You may need to PAD each center with a second layer of RIBBON STITCHES to add dimension.

4. Using light pink 4-mm silk ribbon, stitch LOOPED RIBBON STITCHES, forming edge of center.

5. Using green 9-mm silk ribbon, stitch BULLIONED LAZY DAISY STITCHES, forming leaves.

6. For smaller daisies, cut eleven $2\frac{1}{2}$" lengths of $\frac{1}{4}$" satin ribbon and repeat as above.

Dahlia

1. Cut sixteen 4" lengths of $1\frac{1}{2}$" iridescent wired ribbon. Cut each length as in diagram.

DIAGRAM

2. Fold and pin each ribbon length; see diagram.

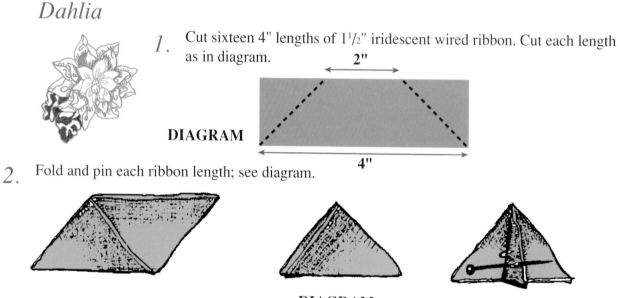

DIAGRAM

3. Place nine pieces side by side and stitch together with a $\frac{1}{4}$" seam allowance using a GATHERING STITCH; see diagram. Pull thread tightly to gather. Connect the first and last petals; secure with stitches; see diagram. Repeat with remaining seven pieces, stitching together with a $\frac{3}{8}$" seam allowance.

DIAGRAM

4. Cut nine $2^1/_4$" lengths of $^5/_8$" peach wired ribbon. Cut each length as in diagram. Repeat Steps 2 and 3.

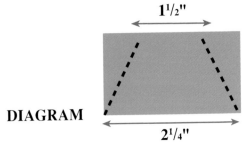

1$^1/_2$"

DIAGRAM

2$^1/_4$"

5. Layer and stitch all gathered chains together from largest to smallest.

6. Cut $^5/_8$" pale green wired ribbon into three 5" lengths. Make three leaves; see Coleus Leaves on page 31. Tuck leaves under dahlia and stitch to secure.

To Finish Bouquet

Swirl and COUCH gold cord to fabric, as shown in photograph. Tie a large fluffy bow with organza ribbon. Stitch in place. Glue charms to bouquet as desired.

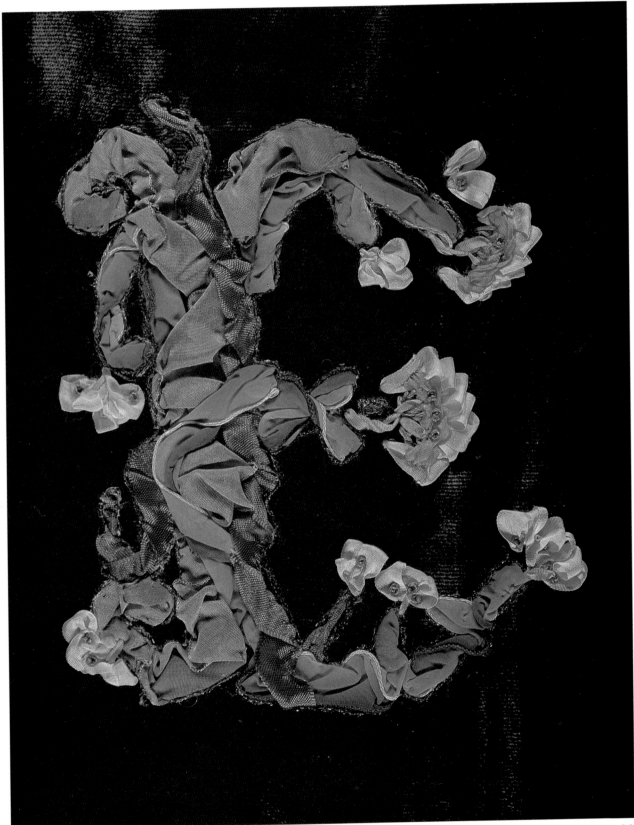

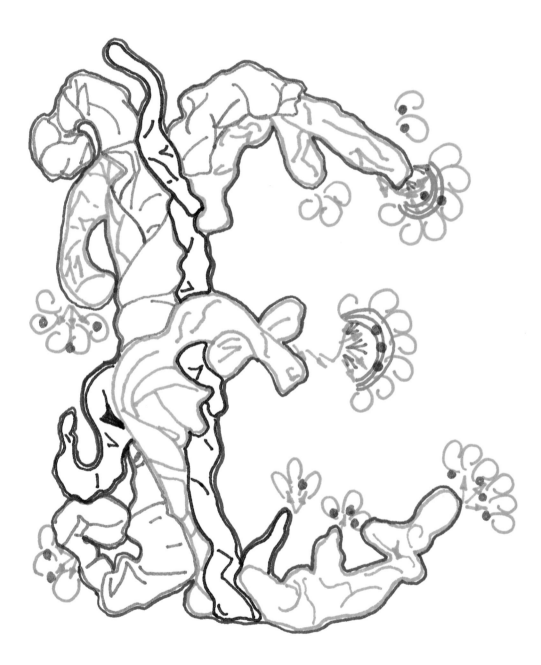

Letter

1. Using three shades of ³/₄" wired ribbon, sculpt and tack ribbons to fabric, forming the letter "E".

2. Outline the letter "E" with metallic gold cord; COUCH to secure.

Evening Primrose

1. Using yellow 7-mm silk ribbon, stitch two or three FRONT LOOPED RIBBON STITCHES, forming buds.

2. Using orange 4-mm silk ribbon, stitch STRAIGHT STITCHES on top of LOOPED RIBBON STITCHES at base.

3. Using green embroidery floss, stitch FRENCH KNOTS on top of LOOPED RIBBON STITCHES above STRAIGHT STITCHES.

4. To make full blooms, stitch six to seven FRONT LOOPED RIBBON STITCHES.

5. Using two shades of orange 4-mm silk ribbon, stitch STRAIGHT STITCHES on top of LOOPED RIBBON STITCHES at base.

6. Using green embroidery floss, stitch FRENCH KNOTS on top of LOOPED RIBBON STITCHES above STRAIGHT STITCHES. Stitch STRAIGHT STITCHES at base of blooms, forming calyx.

Eryingium

1. Using dark purple 4-mm silk ribbon, stitch long RIBBON STITCHES in an acorn shape. Work from the center outward; see diagram.

2. Using light purple 4-mm silk ribbon, stitch long RIBBON STITCHES over previous stitches; see diagram.

3. Using navy 4-mm silk ribbon, stitch long RIBBON STITCHES over previous two shades, yet still allowing all shades to be visible; see diagram.

Step 1   Step 2   Step 3

DIAGRAM

4. Using green 4-mm silk ribbon, stitch ONE-TWIST RIBBON STITCHES under each eryingium, forming calyx.

5. Using three strands of green embroidery floss, stitch STEM STITCHES, forming stems. Using dark green 7-mm silk ribbon, stitch ONE-TWIST RIBBON STITCHES, forming leaves.

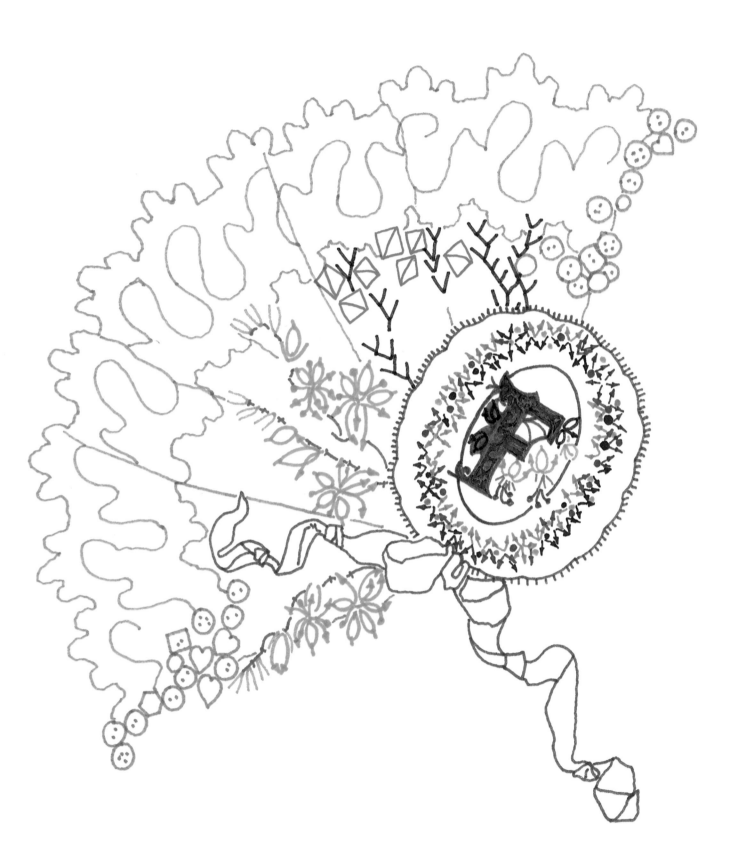

F

Letter

1. Make fan-head pattern. Cut one fan head each from cardboard and fleece. Cut one fan head from fabric, adding ¹/₂" to all edges. Center and paint the letter "F" onto the fabric with fabric paint. Glue fleece to cardboard. Wrap and glue fabric around fleece/cardboard fan head.

2. Using three blue shades and one purple shade of 4-mm silk ribbon, stitch two rows of RIBBON STITCHES around letter, forming oval border. Also stitch FRENCH KNOTS through ribbon stitches. Using pink embroidery floss, stitch FRENCH KNOTS through RIBBON STITCHES. Also, COUCH an oval inside of RIBBON-STITCH oval. Hot-glue braid to outside edge of fan head. Glue handle to fan head.

3. Place an antique piece of lace on fabric in the shape of an open fan; see photo. Tack with invisible thread.

Forget-Me-Nots

Using dark pink 4-mm silk ribbon, stitch RIBBON STITCHES. Using pink embroidery floss, stitch PISTIL STITCHES below RIBBON STITCHES. Using pink 4-mm silk ribbon, stitch LAZY DAISY STITCHES above RIBBON STITCHES. Using green 4-mm silk ribbon, stitch LAZY DAISY STITCHES, forming leaves.

Fuchsias

Using green 4-mm silk ribbon, stitch STEM STITCHES, forming stems. Using dark pink 7-mm silk ribbon, stitch LOOPED RIBBON STITCHES. Tack loops with invisible stitches, forming blooms.

French Knot

Bring needle up at A. Wrap ribbon or floss around needle two times (unless indicated otherwise). Insert needle beside A, pulling ribbon or floss until it fits snugly around needle. Pull needle through to back.

DIAGRAM

Forsythias

1. COUCH green 4-mm silk ribbon to fabric, forming stems. Using dark green 4-mm silk ribbon, stitch STRAIGHT STITCHES, forming leaves. Using yellow 7-mm silk ribbon, stitch BULLIONED LAZY DAISY STITCHES, forming buds.

2. To make full blooms, stitch BULLIONED LAZY DAISY STITCHES placed in a five-spoked shape. Cut three 1^{1}/$_{2}$" lengths of yellow 4-mm silk ribbon. Knot one end of each length. Stitch opposite ends to center of BULLIONED LAZY DAISY STITCHES. Repeat to make five blooms.

To Finish Fan

Glue fan to fabric, over antique lace piece. Tie a bow from ^{3}/$_{4}$" pink wired ribbon. Glue bow to fan handle. CASCADE tails of bow.

Attach buttons and charms as desired.

Fern Stitch

Working from top to bottom of frond, bring needle up at A, down at B. Bring needle up at C, down at A. Bring needle up at D, down again at A. Repeat, until desired length is achieved.

DIAGRAM

Front Looped Ribbon Stitch

Bring needle up through fabric at A. Fold ribbon over itself, creating a loop. Pierce the ribbon with the needle; then take the ribbon down through the fabric.

DIAGRAM

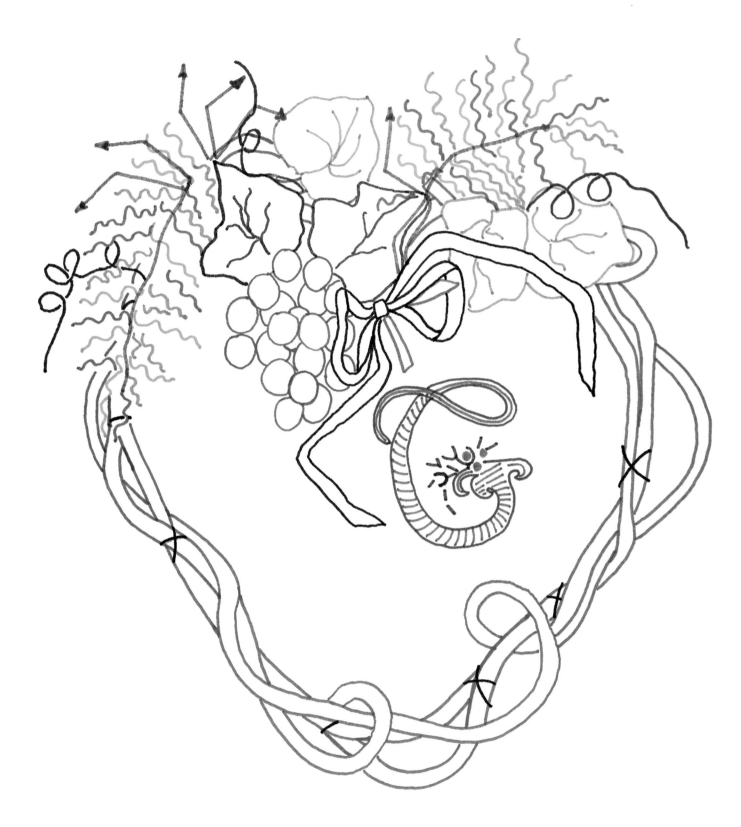

50

G

Letter

1. Using purple embroidery floss, stitch STRAIGHT STITCHES, SATIN-STITCH STYLE, forming the letter "G". Outline letter with RUNNING STITCHES, using brown embroidery floss.

2. Wrap brown cording around fabric, forming a grapevine wreath. COUCH with brown shades of embroidery floss to secure.

3. Place six strands of brown embroidery floss on fabric, forming tendrils. COUCH to secure.

4. After all stitching is completed, tie a bow with brown $^3/_8$" velvet ribbon. Glue bow to center top of grapevine wreath. Tack tails with invisible stitches. Glue charm on center of bow.

Grapes

1. Cut nineteen 1" lengths of purple 1" wired ribbon. Place a pea-sized amount of stuffing in center of length. Wrap ribbon around stuffing. Secure with stitches. Glue grapes to fabric.

2. Cut three 6" lengths each of two green shades of $1^1/_2$" wired ribbon. Make six leaves; see Coleus Leaves on page 31.

Grapevine Flowers

1. COUCH green 4-mm silk ribbon to fabric, forming stems.

2. Using two yellow shades of 7-mm silk ribbon, stitch clusters of SELF SELVAGE GATHERED STITCHES along stems.

3. Using green 7-mm silk ribbon, stitch ONE-TWIST RIBBON STITCHES, forming leaves.

Gardenia

1. Cut thirteen 2" lengths of ⅝" white wired ribbon. Cut lengths as in diagram. Fold, stitch, and gather eight petals, forming bottom layer; see Dahlia on page 36. Repeat, stitching four petals for middle layer and one petal for center. Stitch layers together. Repeat to make two gardenias.

2. Using ⅜" green wired grosgrain ribbon, make five leaves; see Jonquil Leaves on page 66.

1½"

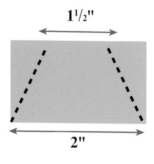

2"

DIAGRAM

54

ℋ

Letter

1. Stitch 4-mm metallic ribbon to fabric, using MJ'S FLUTING STITCH.

2. For the outer border, stitch metallic ribbon at the outer edge of design while randomly swirling the ribbon.

Hydrangea

1. Using four shades of rose 4-mm silk ribbon, stitch RIBBON STITCHES in clusters; see diagram.

2. For the hydrangea leaves, use two shades of green 4-mm silk ribbon. Stitch RIBBON STITCHES to fill the space of each large hydrangea leaf, shading on half of each leaf with the darker shade of ribbon; see diagram.

Step 1

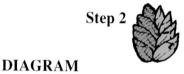

Step 2

DIAGRAM

Honeysuckle

1. Using three strands of green embroidery floss, COUCH to fabric, forming stems.

2. Using light yellow 4-mm silk ribbon, stitch KNOTTED LAZY DAISY STITCHES, forming the large buds of each honeysuckle. Stitch RIBBON STITCHES over the center of the KNOTTED LAZY DAISY STITCHES with yellow 4-mm silk ribbon.

3. Using ivory 4-mm silk ribbon, stitch ONE-TWIST RIBBON STITCHES for the smaller honeysuckles.

4. Using three shades of green 4-mm silk ribbon, stitch LAZY DAISY STITCHES, forming leaves.

5. Bead as desired.

Hollyhock

1. Using light pink 7-mm silk ribbon, stitch STRAIGHT STITCHES; see diagram.

2. Using dark pink 7-mm silk ribbon, stitch RIBBON STITCHES on top of straight stitches; see diagram.

Step 1   **DIAGRAM**   **Step 2**

3. Using both pink shades of 7-mm ribbon, stitch FRENCH KNOTS with two wraps, forming closed buds.

4. Using yellow 4-mm silk ribbon, stitch LOOPED RIBBON STITCHES in centers of hollyhocks.

Rosettes

Using two pink shades of 4-mm silk ribbon, make ROSETTES; see Rosettes on page 116.

Herringbone-Style Stitch

The herringbone-style stitch is a pleasing pattern for a border design. Bring needle up through fabric at A, then back down through fabric at B. Up through fabric at C, then down through fabric at D. Continue in this manner until desired length is achieved.

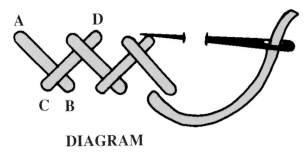

DIAGRAM

Heather

1. Using four shades of rose 4-mm silk ribbon, stitch FRENCH KNOTS.

2. Using green 4-mm silk ribbon, stitch RIBBON STITCHES throughout FRENCH KNOTS, forming leaves.

59

Letter

1. Using 9-mm silk ribbon, stitch STRAIGHT STITCHES, SATIN-STITCH STYLE, forming the letter "I".

2. Using purple 4-mm silk ribbon, weave the ribbon in and out of the STRAIGHT STITCHES, cinching in the top and bottoms of the STRAIGHT STITCH with the 4-mm silk ribbon. Weave the 4-mm silk ribbon again through the first weaving to add the outer texture to the letter "I".

3. To make vine, COUCH light green embroidery floss, encircling the letter "I". Weave a darker shade of embroidery floss through COUCHING.

4. Using dark green 4-mm silk ribbon, stitch RIBBON STITCHES along vine, forming leaves.

Iris Flower

1. To make stem, cut a 6" length of $^3/_8$" green wired ribbon. Twist ribbon to form a coil; pin in place. Stitch coiled ribbon to fabric with invisible thread. Repeat to make a second stem.

2. Cut a 6" length of narrow green cording. Untwist. COUCH each untwisted length to either side of the stem. Repeat on remaining stem.

3. Cut a 12$^1/_2$" length and an 8$^1/_2$" length of $^7/_8$" ombré purple wired ribbon. Beginning and ending $^1/_4$" from ends, mark each length at 4" intervals; see diagram. (Note: Ribbon is reversed for smaller length.) Stitch a GATHERING STITCH following blue stitching lines. Pull thread tightly to gather; secure thread with stitches.

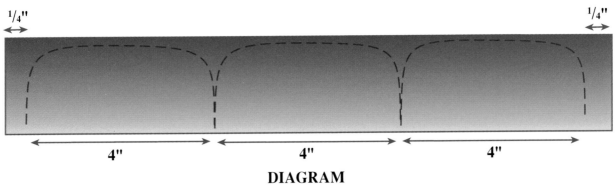

DIAGRAM

4. Pin the three-petaled length to the fabric. Fold the two outer petals outward and in half; see diagram. Stitch to the fabric with invisible stitches, allowing the petals to ruffle. Pin the two-petaled length to the fabric above three-petaled length. Fold bottom half of each petal upward. Stitch with invisible stitches, allowing the petals to ruffle.

5. Using yellow 4-mm silk ribbon, stitch two SELF SELVAGE GATHERED STITCHES, below the top of the two-petaled length.

6. Repeat Steps 3 and 4 to make a second iris.

Ivy

1. Using two strands each of two shades of brown embroidery floss, stitch stems; COUCH to secure.

2. Using three shades of green 4-mm silk ribbon, stitch a BULLION LAZY DAISY STITCH with a RIBBON STITCH on each side, forming leaves.

Impatiens

1. Using two green shades of 7-mm silk ribbon, stitch RIBBON STITCHES, forming greenery.

2. Using three shades of 4-mm silk ribbon, stitch FRONT-LOOPED RIBBON STITCHES in a five-spoked shape. Stitch a LOOPED RIBBON STITCH in the center of each spoke shape with white 4-mm silk ribbon. Stitch LAZY DAISY STITCHES, alternating colors, to form buds.

Letter

Using bugle beads and seed beads, bead the letter "J".

Jonquil Leaves

Cut ⁵/₈" dark green wired ribbon into eight 3¹/₄" lengths. Fold lengths as in diagram. Stitch a GATHERING STITCH at bottom edge of folded ribbon with a ¹/₄" seam allowance. Wrap the thread around the ribbon twice; secure. Repeat using seven 2¹/₂" lengths of ³/₈" light green wired ribbon. Stitch leaves in place. Randomly stitch pearls within the leaves.

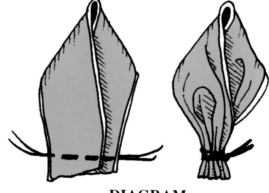

DIAGRAM

Jonquil Flower

1. Cut 1¹/₂" yellow wired ribbon into six 4" lengths. Cut lengths as shown in diagram. Fold, stitch, and gather the petals as for the Dahlia; see Dahlia on page 36.

DIAGRAM

2¹/₂"

4¹/₂"

2. Connect the first and last petals together. Stitch the petals over the leaves. Turn the tip of each petal back, slightly squaring the petal; tack.

3. Cut a 6" length of 1¹/₂" yellow wired ribbon. Fold ribbon in half lengthwise; see diagram. Fold the ribbon in half, matching short ends; see diagram. Stitch a ¹/₄" seam. Turn seam inward.

4. Stitch a GATHERING STITCH along folded edge; see diagram. Pull thread tightly to gather. Place in center of chained gathered petals. Glue artificial stamens in center.

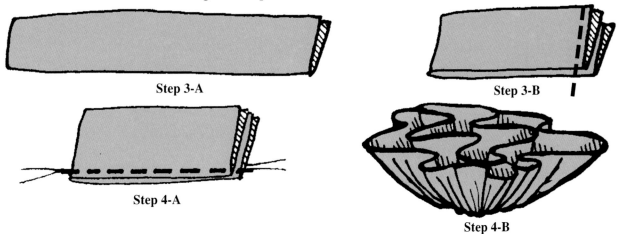

Step 3-A

Step 3-B

Step 4-A

Step 4-B

DIAGRAM

Jasmine Flowers

1. Using ivory 4-mm silk ribbon, stitch BULLIONED LAZY DAISY STITCHES placed in a five-spoke shape, forming jasmine petals.

2. Using green 4-mm silk ribbon, stitch BULLIONED LAZY DAISY STITCHES, forming buds; see diagram.

3. Using green 4-mm silk ribbon, interweave ribbon throughout buds, forming vine; see diagram.

4. Using two shades of green 4-mm silk ribbon, stitch RIBBON STITCHES encircling the jasmine flowers, forming leaves. Stitch pearls where desired.

DIAGRAM

Johnny Jump-Ups

1. Randomly alternating seven shades of 4-mm silk ribbon, make johnny jump-ups.

2. Using one shade of 4-mm silk ribbon, stitch three STRAIGHT STITCHES, forming bottom of flower; see diagram.

3. Using a second shade of 4-mm silk ribbon, stitch four RIBBON STITCHES, as shown in diagram, to form the top of the flower.

4. Using a third shade of 4-mm silk ribbon, stitch a RIBBON STITCH on each side of the flower, forming leaves; see diagram.

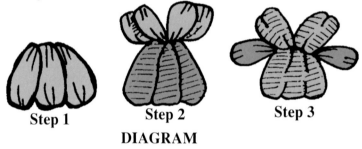

Step 1   Step 2   Step 3

DIAGRAM

5. Using one strand of embroidery floss, stitch STRAIGHT STITCHES on the bottom half of each flower. Weave green embroidery floss through flowers, forming vines. COUCH as necessary. Using green 4-mm silk ribbon, stitch a BULLIONED LAZY DAISY STITCH, forming center of leaves. Stitch a RIBBON STITCH to one side of the BULLIONED LAZY DAISY STITCH. Using dark green 4-mm silk ribbon, stitch RIBBON STITCHES, forming small leaves.

K

Letter

1. Using ivory 7-mm silk ribbon, lay lengths side by side, forming letter box. Tack with small stitches.

2. Border edges of box with gold 7-mm silk ribbon, covering raw edges.

3. Using gold embroidery floss, stitch BUTTONHOLE STITCHES along outside edge of box.

4. Using brown embroidery floss, stitch STRAIGHT STITCHES, SATIN-STITCH STYLE, forming the letter "K".

Kelatios

1. Using green 7-mm silk ribbon, stitch large RIBBON STITCHES, forming leaves. Stitch smaller leaves, using green 4-mm silk ribbon and stitching small RIBBON STITCHES.

2. Using green 4-mm silk ribbon, stitch STEM STITCHES, forming stems.

3. Using pink embroidery floss, stitch LAZY DAISY STITCHES, placed in a five-spoked shape, forming flowers

Fuchsias

1. Using two shades of pink and one shade of yellow 7-mm silk ribbon, stitch fuchsias; see Fuchsias on page 46.

2. Using two shades of pink and one shade of yellow 4-mm silk ribbon, stitch FRENCH KNOT clusters around fuchsias.

Knotted Lazy Daisy Stitch

Make a LAZY DAISY loop, then turn the fabric so that the top of the loop is facing you. Wrap ribbon two times around needle, as for a FRENCH KNOT. Insert needle into fabric in the same place as you would for the anchor stitch of the LAZY DAISY. Push wraps down the needle to meet the fabric. Pull needle gently through to the underside.

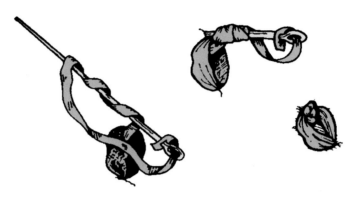

DIAGRAM

76

L

Letter

Using coral 4-mm silk ribbon, stitch RIBBON STITCHES, SATIN-STITCH STYLE, forming the letter "L". Outline letter with RUNNING STITCHES; see diagram. Stitch swirls with running stitches. Weave the coral ribbon in and out of the RUNNING STITCHES; see diagram. Double-weave the RUNNING STITCHES with gold thread; see diagram.

Larkspur

1. Using rose 4-mm silk ribbon, stitch CRISSCROSSED LAZY DAISY STITCHES; see diagram.

2. Using two different shades of rose 4-mm silk ribbon, stitch RIBBON STITCHES around the CRISSCROSSED LAZY DAISIES; see diagram.

DIAGRAM

Lavender

1. Using two gray shades of 4-mm silk ribbon, stitch RIBBON STITCHES, HERRINGBONE-STYLE.

2. Weave green 4-mm silk ribbon in and out of HERRINGBONE-STYLE RIBBON STITCHES to form stems; COUCH to secure.

Lobelia

1. For a full-blooming lobelia, stitch three long RIBBON STITCHES, then two short RIBBON STITCHES, randomly alternating three blue shades of 4-mm silk ribbon; see diagram. For half-blooming lobelia, stitch only two RIBBON STITCHES. Stitch a 2¹/₂" pearl in center of each lobelia; see diagram

DIAGRAM

2. Weave green 4-mm silk ribbon through petals of lobelia to form the stem.

3. For Lobelia bud, stitch two wrapped FRENCH KNOTS, using two shades of blue 4-mm silk ribbon.

Lily of the Valley

1. Using white 4-mm silk ribbon, stitch BULLIONED LAZY DAISY STITCHES, forming flowers; see diagram.

DIAGRAM

2. Using six strands each of two green shades of embroidery floss, stitch stems, using the STEM STITCH.

3. Using 15-mm metallic-trimmed sheer ribbon, stitch two very large ONE-TWIST RIBBON STITCHES, to make leaves.

Lazy Daisy Stitch

Bring needle up through fabric at A. Insert needle back into fabric right next to A and bring needle out again at B (about ¹/₄" from A). Turn ribbon and slip under tip of needle, keeping ribbon flat. Hold loop down with thumb, while pulling ribbon through, to close the loop. Insert needle back into fabric at top as a tack stitch. The length of the LAZY DAISY STITCH can be varied.

DIAGRAM

Looped Ribbon Stitch

Flatten the ribbon toward you, pierce the ribbon only with the needle tip, and move the needle tip back toward the ribbon's entry point; then take the needle down through the fabric. This forms a loop that sits above the fabric.

DIAGRAM

Long One-Twist Ribbon Stitch

See One-Twist Ribbon Stitch on page 95.

Lilacs

1. Using six lavender shades of 4-mm silk ribbon, stitch LAZY DAISY STITCHES, randomly alternating shades.

2. Using two shades of green 4-mm silk ribbon, stitch RIBBON STITCHES within each lilac cluster, forming leaves.

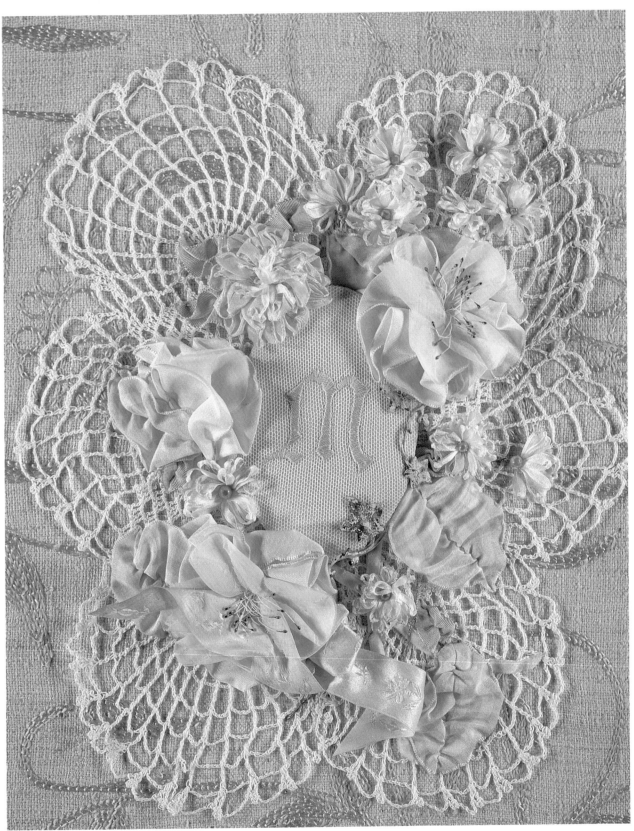

M

Letter

Using ivory silk embroidery floss, stitch SATIN STITCHES, forming the letter "M".

Magnolia

1. Cut a 16" length of 1½" ivory wired ribbon. Mark ribbon as in diagram. Fold ribbon in diagonals at marks, securing with pins; see diagram. Stitch short ends together; see diagram.

2. Stitch a GATHERING STITCH along inside edge; see diagram. Pull tightly to gather, forming bottom layer of large magnolia.

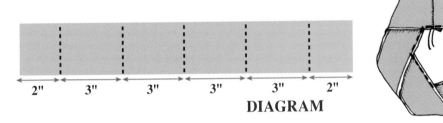

| 2" | 3" | 3" | 3" | 3" | 2" |

DIAGRAM

3. For bottom layer of small magnolia, repeat Steps 1 and 2 with a 10" length of 1½" ivory wired ribbon and marking according to diagram.

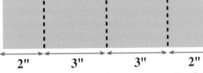

| 2" | 3" | 3" | 2" |

DIAGRAM

4. Cut fourteen petals from organdy fabric. Curl outer edges of each petal around a toothpick; see diagram. Stitch ten curled petals together with a GATHERING STITCH. Pull thread tightly to gather. Secure thread. Join the first and last petals. Stitch gathered petals on top of bottom layer of large magnolia. Join remaining four petals as above; stitch on top of bottom layer of small magnolia. Fold artificial stamens in half and stitch to center of each flower.

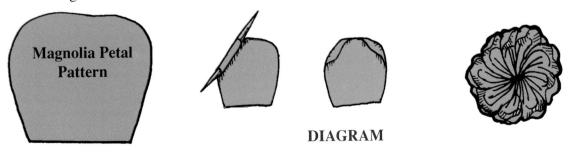

Magnolia Petal Pattern

DIAGRAM

5. Cut five 7" lengths of 1" ivory striped wired ribbon. Make a leaf; see Coleus Leaves on page 31. Repeat with three 2½" lengths of ⅜" tan grosgrain ribbon to make small leaves.

6. Place ³⁄₁₆" velvet ribbon on fabric, forming stems. COUCH to secure.

Marigold Flower

1. Cut a 23" length and a 20" length of 1" wired ribbon. Beginning and ending ¼" from ends, mark each ribbon strip at 1⅜" intervals. GATHER-STITCH each length of ribbon, following blue stitching lines; see diagram. Pull thread to gather petals. Connect first and last petals, securing with stitches. Stitch the smaller gathered length on top of the larger gathered length.

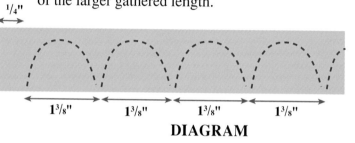

¼"

1⅜"   1⅜"   1⅜"   1⅜"

DIAGRAM

2. To make stamens, tie thirteen knots spaced 1½" apart in a length of ivory 4-mm silk ribbon. Cut ribbon apart just past each knot. Fold lengths in half. Place the knotted lengths side by side. Stitch knotted ends of the lengths together with a GATHERING STITCH. Join the first and last lengths. Stitch to center of gathered layer. Stitch the stamens in center of marigold.

3. For marigold leaves, cut three 4" lengths of ⅜" tan grosgrain ribbon. Make leaves; see Coleus Leaves on page 31.

Marguerite

1. Cut seven 2" lengths each of three shades of 4-mm silk ribbon. Tie a knot in center of each length. Fold lengths in half. Place lengths side by side and sew together with GATHERING STITCHES; see diagram. Pull thread to gather. Join the first and last lengths. Attach to fabric. Stitch pearls at center of flowers.

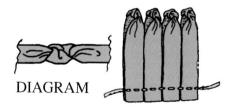

DIAGRAM

2. For small marguerite, cut four 2" lengths each of two shades of ivory and three 2" lengths of an additional shade of ivory 4-mm silk ribbon. Complete flower as above.

Morning Glories

1. Using blue 4-mm silk ribbon, stitch RIBBON STITCHES placed in a five-spoke shape, forming bottom layer of flower; see diagram.

2. Using blue 4-mm silk ribbon, stitch STRAIGHT STITCHES between RIBBON STITCHES; see diagram.

Step 1   **DIAGRAM**   Step 2

3. Using light blue 4-mm silk ribbon, stitch RIBBON STITCHES slightly inward and on top of previous stitches; see diagram.

4. Using white 4-mm silk ribbon, stitch ONE-TWIST RIBBON STITCHES; see diagram.

Step 3   Step 4

DIAGRAM

5. Using yellow 4-mm silk ribbon, stitch a LOOPED RIBBON STITCH, forming the center of each large morning glory.

6. To make buds, stitch four RIBBON STITCHES with blue 4-mm silk ribbon; see diagram.

7. Using green 4-mm silk ribbon, stitch STRAIGHT STITCHES across the top of each bud, cinching the RIBBON STITCHES; see diagram.

8. Using dark green 4-mm silk ribbon, stitch a BULLIONED LAZY DAISY STITCH for the center of each leaf. Stitch RIBBON STITCHES on each side; see diagram.

Step 6   Step 7   Step 8

DIAGRAM

9. Place cording on fabric, forming stems. COUCH to secure.

MJ's Fluting

Fold the ribbon diagonally back and forth, forming a continuous series of mountain-shaped folds.

DIAGRAM

MJ's Twisty Rose

Bring needle up at A. Extend ribbon its full length and twirl needle, so that the ribbon coils, but not so tight that it buckles. Gently hold the ribbon at about the midpoint and insert the needle back into the fabric a short distance from A. Pull the needle through until only the eye sticks up through the fabric. Release the ribbon and it will automatically twist back on itself. Gently smooth the entire length of the twisted ribbon and pull the needle through to the under-side. The ribbon will magically bunch up into a rose as you pull the ribbon through the fabric. Allow some of the bunched ribbon to remain on the surface as a Twisty Rose. Take another stitch up through the rose and back down again to tack the rose secure. Use matching thread to make tiny tack stitches to secure the outer petals to the fabric.

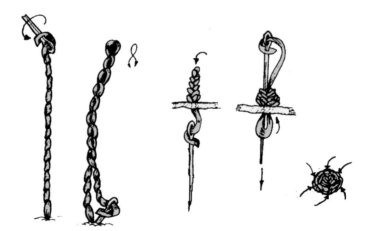

DIAGRAM

89

Letter

1. COUCH one shade of green 4-mm silk ribbon to fabric, forming vines and the letter "N".

2. Using a second shade of green 4-mm silk ribbon, stitch RIBBON STITCHES along vines, forming leaves.

3. Using shades of gold and rose 4-mm silk ribbon, stitch LAZY DAISY STITCHES along vines, forming buds.

4. Using rose shades of 4-mm silk ribbon, make rosettes; see Rosettes on page 116. Stitch rosettes along vines. Using green 7-mm silk ribbon, stitch a SELF-SELVAGE GATHERED STITCH around base of each rosette.

Narcissus

1. Using tan 4-mm silk ribbon, stitch LAZY DAISY STITCHES, placed in a five-spoke shape.

2. Using yellow 4-mm silk ribbon, stitch FRENCH KNOTS at centers of spokes.

3. Using ivory 4-mm silk ribbon, wrap FRENCH KNOT centers twice; secure with small stitches.

Hollyhock

Using two shades of purple 4-mm silk ribbon, stitch hollyhocks along vines; see Hollyhocks on page 57.

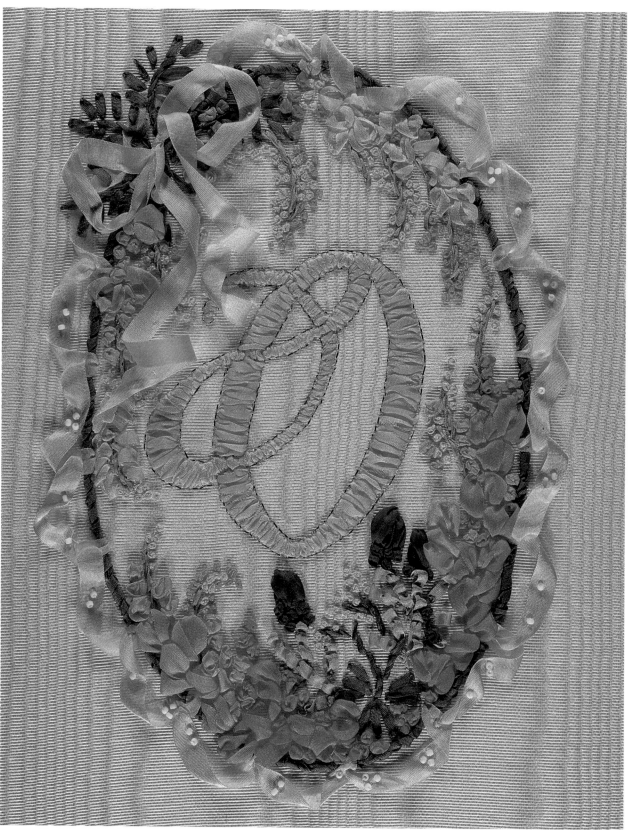

93

Letter

1. Using yellow 4-mm silk ribbon, stitch STRAIGHT STITCHES, SATIN-STITCH STYLE, forming the letter "O". Outline letter with RUNNING STITCHES, using metallic gold thread.

2. Using 4-mm silk ribbon, stitch RUNNING STITCHES, forming oval border. Weave ribbon through RUNNING STITCHES; see diagram.

DIAGRAM

3. Using green 4-mm silk ribbon, stitch FERN STITCHES.

4. Tie a bow with peach 7-mm silk ribbon. CASCADE tails around oval. Stitch white seed beads around CASCADING.

Obedient Flowers

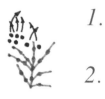

1. Using light green 4-mm silk ribbon, stitch STEM STITCHES, forming stems.

2. Using three shades of pink 4-mm and 7-mm silk ribbon, stitch LAZY DAISY STITCHES and FRENCH KNOTS around stems.

Owl's Cover

1. Using light green 4-mm silk ribbon, stitch a chain of FRONT LOOPED RIBBON STITCHES to form stems.

2. Using 4-mm burgundy silk ribbon, stitch FRENCH KNOTS above stems.

3. Using 4-mm burgundy silk ribbon, stitch STRAIGHT STITCHES above FRENCH KNOTS.

One-Twist Ribbon Stitch

Bring ribbon up through fabric. Twist ribbon one time, and complete ribbon stitch.

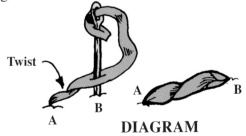

DIAGRAM

One-Twist Ribbon Stitch (Long)

Bring ribbon up through fabric. Extend ribbon to the length of the desired stitch. Twist ribbon one time, complete ribbon stitch. At the point where the ribbon is twisted, invisibly tack the stitch in the crease to hold stitch in place.

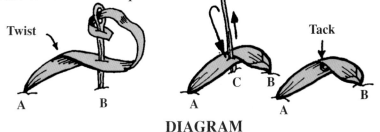

DIAGRAM

Letter

1. Using green 4-mm silk ribbon, stitch RIBBON STITCHES, SATIN-STITCH STYLE, forming the letter "P".

2. Using 1" wired ribbon, tie a bow. Stitch to fabric.

Poinsettias

1. Using a dark shade of red 4-mm silk ribbon, stitch BULLIONED LAZY DAISY STITCHES, placed in a five-spoke shape. Fill between stitches with more BULLIONED LAZY DAISY STITCHES; see diagram. (For the largest poinsettia, begin the bottom layer of petals with 8-mm silk ribbon.)

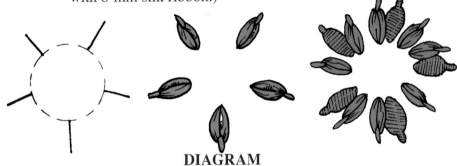

DIAGRAM

2. Repeat Step 1, stitching a second layer of BULLIONED LAZY DAISY STITCHES closer to the center than the previous layer, alternating between two lighter shades of red; see diagram.

3. Using medium shade of red, stitch ONE-TWIST RIBBON STITCHES, forming top layer; see diagram.

4. Using gold 4-mm silk ribbon, stitch LOOPED RIBBON STITCHES, forming center of each poinsettia.

Step 2   **Step 3**   **Step 4**

DIAGRAM

Pepper Berries

Using three shades of 4-mm silk ribbon, stitch FRENCH KNOTS with two and three knots.

Pine Cones

Cut a 12" length each of two brown shades of 4-mm silk ribbon. Thread both lengths through a size 1 crewel embroidery needle. Stitch a MJ'S TWISTY ROSE, allowing most of the bunched ribbon to remain on the surface of the fabric. Lay the bunched ribbon over on its side and shape as a pine cone. Tack the tip of each pine cone in place.

Pine Boughs

1. Using two strands of green embroidery floss, stitch STRAIGHT STITCHES to form pine boughs.

2. Using two strands of a lighter shade of embroidery floss, stitch STRAIGHT STITCHES over the previous stitches to shade.

Pansies

1. Cut a 9" length of ⁵⁄₈" lavender wired ombré ribbon. Beginning and ending ¹⁄₄" from ends, mark a 2¹⁄₄" interval, a 4" interval and a 2¹⁄₄" interval; see diagram.

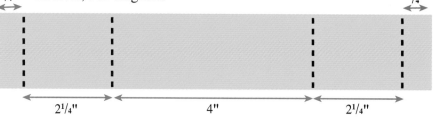

¹⁄₄"   ¹⁄₄"

2¹⁄₄"   4"   2¹⁄₄"

2. Fold ribbon at marks. Stitch a GATHERING STITCH beginning on the inside bottom edge; see diagram. Pull thread tightly to gather. Stitch raw ends together; secure thread. Repeat to make two rose pansies and two purple pansies.

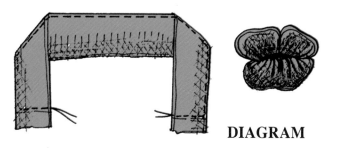

DIAGRAM

100

3. To make two-petaled buds, cut a 5" length of ⁵/₈" lavender wired ombré ribbon. Beginning and ending ¹/₄" from ends, mark 2¹/₄" intervals; see diagram. Fold ribbon at marks and stitch a GATHERING STITCH; see diagram. Repeat to make two rose buds and a purple bud.

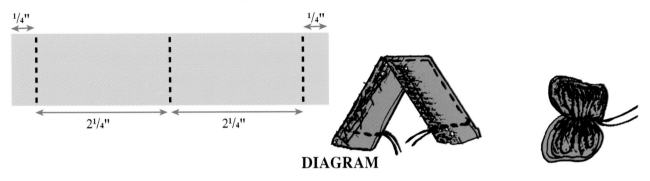

DIAGRAM

4. To make one-petaled buds, cut a 2³/₄" length of lavender wired ombré ribbon. Stitch a GATHERING STITCH as shown in diagram. Pull thread tightly to gather; secure thread. Repeat to make a rose bud and a purple bud.

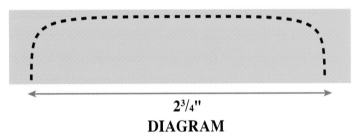

2³/₄"

DIAGRAM

5. Using 4-mm silk ribbon, stitch STRAIGHT STITCHES at bases of pansy buds. Stitch RIBBON STITCHES onto the body of the buds, forming the calyx.

6. Using three green shades of embroidery floss, make eight 4" coiled floss lengths. Stitch the lengths in place with invisible stitches, forming stems.

Pistil Stitch

Insert needle through fabric at A and lift a length of floss or ribbon to B. Lay the floss down to the fabric and make a FRENCH KNOT at B, using one to two wraps for the knot. Take the needle back down through the fabric.

DIAGRAM

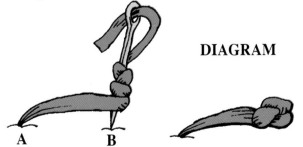

A   B

Peonies

1. Using light rose 7-mm silk ribbon, stitch a BULLIONED LAZY DAISY STITCH to form the center of the peony. Stitch three RIBBON STITCHES on each side of the BULLIONED LAZY DAISY STITCH; see diagram.

2. Alternating three shades of coral 4-mm silk ribbon, stitch TWISTED RIBBON STITCHES between previous stitches; see diagram.

3. Using light coral 4-mm silk ribbon, stitch RIBBON STITCHES to form the bottom half of the peony; see diagram.

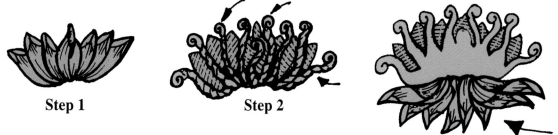

Step 1   Step 2   Step 3

DIAGRAM

4. Using bright coral 4-mm silk ribbon, stitch ONE-TWIST RIBBON STITCHES between RIBBON STITCHES.

5. Using two shades of green 7-mm silk ribbon, stitch BULLIONED LAZY DAISY STITCHES and LAZY DAISY STITCHES to form leaves.

Padded Stitch

This technique creates an effect that adds dimension and texture to designs. Simply layer like stitches on top of one another, working stitches close together so that little or no fabric shows from underneath.

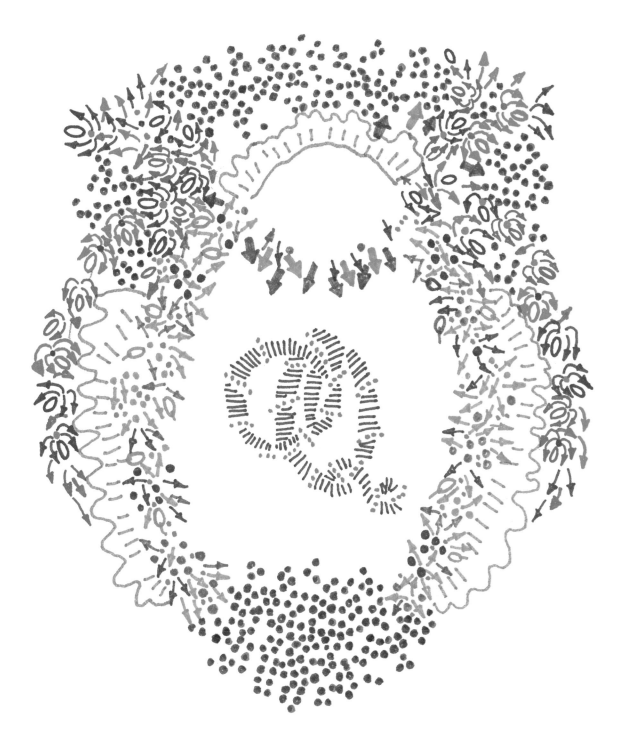

Letter

1. Using mauve 4-mm silk ribbon, stitch RIBBON STITCHES, SATIN-STITCH STYLE to form the letter "Q".

2. Stitch assorted seed beads to letter where indicated.

3. Mark embroidery for placement of porcelain angel or desired charm. Using 7-mm silk ribbon, stitch RIBBON STITCHES around markings.

Queen of the Meadow

1. Using three shades of pink 4-mm silk ribbon, randomly stitch FRENCH KNOTS and RIBBON STITCHES to form flowers; see diagram.

DIAGRAM

2. Using two shades of green 4-mm silk ribbon, randomly stitch BULLIONED LAZY DAISY STITCHES and RIBBON STITCHES to form leaves.

3. Stitch assorted seed beads throughout.

Queen's Wreath

1. Using two strands of green embroidery floss, stitch STEM STITCHES to form stems.

2. Using one shade of pink 4-mm silk ribbon, stitch LAZY DAISY STITCHES to form center of each flower.

3. Using a second shade of pink 4-mm silk ribbon, stitch RIBBON STITCHES on each side of LAZY DAISY STITCHES to form a heart shaped flower. Stitch beads as desired.

Queen Anne's Lace

Using white 4-mm silk ribbon, stitch FRENCH KNOTS. Stitch seed beads throughout.

Glue porcelain angel or charm in place to complete.

R

Letter

1. Using rose silk embroidery floss, stitch SATIN STITCHES to form the letter "R".

2. Using two shades of pink 4-mm silk ribbon, stitch FRENCH KNOTS on the letter "R".

3. Using two shades of green 4-mm silk ribbon, stitch RIBBON STITCHES, LAZY DAISY STITCHES and BULLIONED LAZY DAISY STITCHES to form leaves.

Rose of the Year Rose Cluster

1. Cut an 8¹/₂" length of red 7-mm silk ribbon. Beginning and ending ¹/₄" from ends, mark ribbon at 1" intervals, as shown in diagram. GATHER- STITCH each length of ribbon, following the blue stitching line; see diagram. Pull thread tightly to gather. Connect the first and last petals. Secure with stitches. Hand-stitch to fabric.

2. Using dark red 4-mm silk ribbon, stitch a MJ'S TWISTY ROSE at center of eight-petaled flower; see diagram.

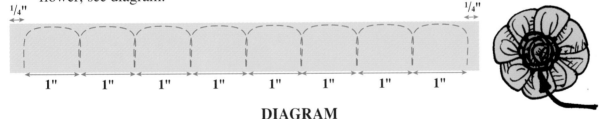

¹/₄"   ¹/₄"

1"   1"   1"   1"   1"   1"   1"   1"

DIAGRAM

3. To make smaller rose, stitch a MJ'S TWISTY ROSE, using bright red 4-mm silk ribbon, to form center. Alternately stitch RIBBON STITCHES around rose with dark red and coral rose 4-mm silk ribbons.

4. Using coral rose 4-mm silk ribbon, stitch KNOTTED LAZY DAISY STITCHES to form buds.

5. Using green 4-mm silk ribbon, stitch RIBBON STITCHES and BULLIONED LAZY DAISY STITCHES to form leaves.

Simplicity Rose Cluster

1. Using one shade of rose 4-mm silk ribbon, stitch three BULLION STITCHES; see diagram.

2. Using a second shade of rose 4-mm silk ribbon, stitch three BULLION STITCHES around the previous stitches; see diagram.

3. Using a third shade of rose 4-mm silk ribbon, stitch two BULLION STITCHES around previous stitches; see diagram.

4. Using a fourth shade of rose 4-mm silk ribbon, stitch a SELF SELVAGE GATHERED STITCH around BULLION STITCHES; see diagram.

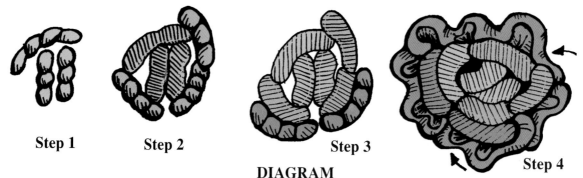

Step 1   **Step 2**   **Step 3**   **Step 4**

DIAGRAM

5. To make large buds, stitch BULLION STITCHES, using two shades of rose 4-mm silk ribbon. Edge with a SELF SELVAGE GATHERED RUFFLE, using pink 4-mm silk ribbon.

6. To make small buds, stitch LAZY DAISY STITCHES using orchid 4-mm silk ribbon.

7. Using two shades of green 4-mm silk ribbon, stitch BULLION LAZY DAISY STITCHES and RIBBON STITCHES, forming leaves.

Touch of Class Rose Cluster

1. Using light pink ribbon, stitch a BULLIONED LAZY DAISY STITCH to form the center of the rose. Alternating three shades of pink 4-mm silk ribbon, stitch RIBBON STITCHES and ONE TWIST RIBBON STITCHES around center; see diagram.

DIAGRAM

2. Stitch large and small buds in the same fashion, randomly alternating shades of ribbon.

3. Using two green shades of 4-mm silk ribbon, stitch BULLIONED LAZY DAISY STITCHES and RIBBON STITCHES, forming leaves.

Harmony Rose Cluster

1. Cut a 12¹/₂" length of one shade of pink 13-mm silk ribbon. Beginning and ending ¹/₄" from ends, mark ribbon at 1¹/₂" intervals; see diagram. Stitch a GATHERING STITCH, following the blue stitching line; see diagram. Pull thread tightly to gather; secure with stitches. Connect the first and last petals.

DIAGRAM

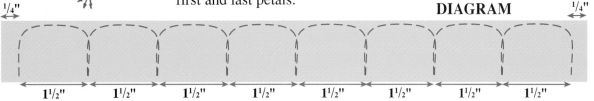

¹/₄"   ¹/₄"

1¹/₂"   1¹/₂"   1¹/₂"   1¹/₂"   1¹/₂"   1¹/₂"   1¹/₂"   1¹/₂"

2. Cut a 7" length of a lighter shade of 7-mm silk ribbon. Short ends together. Stitch a GATHERING STITCH along one edge. Pull thread tightly to gather; secure with stitches. Stitch on top of the eight-petaled flower. Using the lightest shade of 7-mm silk ribbon, stitch a MJ'S TWISTY ROSE at center of layers.

3. To make small rose, cut an 8¹/₂" length each of rose 7-mm silk ribbon and pink organdy ³/₈" ribbon. Layer the two ribbons together. Stitch and gather ribbons; see Rose of the Year Rose Cluster. Stitch a gathering stitch along one edge of a 5" length of pink 4-mm silk ribbon. Stitch on top of eight-petaled flower. Stitch a MJ'S TWISTY ROSE at center of flower.

4. Using green 4-mm silk ribbon, stitch BULLIONED LAZY DAISY STITCHES, to form leaves.

Lexi's Rose Cluster

1. Using purple embroidery floss, stitch STRAIGHT STITCHES, placed in a five spoke shape; see diagram.

2. Using dark purple 4-mm silk ribbon, weave ribbon under and over the spokes. Let the ribbon remain loose as you weave. Cover almost half of the length of the spokes; then switch to a slightly lighter shade of ribbon. Continue until three shades of ribbon have covered the spokes.

DIAGRAM

113

3. Repeat Steps 1 and 2 to make three roses.

4. To make bud, stitch two BULLION STITCHES with lightest shade of 4-mm silk ribbon.

5. Using 4-mm green silk ribbon, stitch BULLION LAZY DAISY STITCHES and RIBBON STITCHES to form leaves.

Claire's Rose Cluster

1. Using two shades of red 4-mm silk ribbon, stitch FRONT LOOPED RIBBON STITCHES to form the outer edge of the circle; see diagram.

2. Using a medium shade of red 4-mm silk ribbon, stitch a SELF SELVAGE GATHERED STITCH inward from FRONT LOOPED RIBBON STITCHES; see diagram.

3. Using a dark shade of red 4-mm silk ribbon, stitch a MJ'S TWISTY ROSE at center; see diagram. Repeat Steps 1–3 to make an additional rose.

DIAGRAM

Step 1 Step 2 Step 3

4. To make buds, stitch a KNOTTED LAZY DAISY STITCH, using dark red 4-mm silk ribbon. Stitch RIBBON STITCHES on each side; see diagram. Repeat to make three buds.

DIAGRAM

5. Using two green shades of 4-mm silk ribbon, stitch BULLIONED LAZY DAISY STITCHES and RIBBON STITCHES to form leaves.

Radiant Rose Cluster

1. Cut a 5" length of 13-mm silk ribbon. Stitch ends together, forming a tube. Stitch a GATHERING STITCH along one edge of tube. Pull thread tightly to gather; secure with stitches. Stitch to fabric.

2. Cut a 5" length of 7-mm silk ribbon and repeat as above.

3. Cut two 7" lengths of two shades of 7-mm silk ribbon. Layer ribbons together and make a rosette.

4. To make buds, use three shades of red 4-mm silk ribbon; see Touch of Class Rose Cluster.

5. Using green 4-mm silk ribbon, stitch BULLIONED LAZY DAISY STITCHES, forming leaves.

Cottage Rose Cluster

1. Using two shades of pink 4-mm silk ribbon, stitch two layers of CROSSOVER LOOPED RIBBON STITCHES; see diagram.

2. Using lavender 4-mm silk ribbon, stitch a MJ'S TWISTY ROSE at center of CROSSOVER LOOPED RIBBON STITCHES; see diagram.

Step 1

Step 2

DIAGRAM

3. Cut a 9" length of ³/₈" pink organdy ribbon. Stitch short ends together. Stitch a GATHERING STITCH along one edge of the ribbon. Pull thread tightly to gather. Stitch under CROSS-OVER LOOPED RIBBON STITCH layers.

4. Using pink 7-mm silk ribbon, stitch LAZY DAISY STITCHES, forming buds. Add smaller buds using coral 4-mm silk ribbon.

5. Using green 4-mm silk ribbon, stitch BULLIONED LAZY DAISY STITCHES and RIBBON STITCHES to form leaves.

Love's Red Rose Cluster

1. Cut a 12¹/₂" length of ¹/₂" grosgrain ribbon. Stitch and gather; see Harmony Rose Cluster.

2. Make a rosette from 9-mm silk ribbon. Cut a 9" length of ³/₈" burgundy organdy ribbon. Gather ribbon around rosette. Stitch to center of eight-petaled rose.

3. Cut a 12" length of 1" wired ombré ribbon. Fold ribbon in half, matching long edges; see diagram. Stitch a GATHERING STITCH along wired edges; see diagram. Pull thread tightly to gather. Join the ends together; secure with stitches. Stitch under eight-petaled rose.

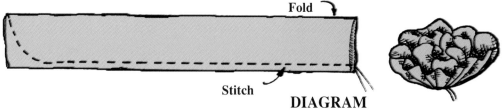

DIAGRAM

4. To make buds, fold and stitch 13-mm silk ribbon as shown in diagram. Using green 4-mm silk ribbon, stitch over the base of the buds with STRAIGHT STITCHES.

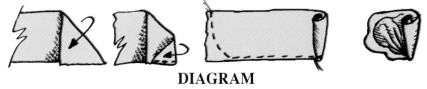

DIAGRAM

5. To make stems, stitch long ONE-TWIST RIBBON STITCHES, using green 4-mm silk ribbon.

Ribbon Stitch

Bring needle up through fabric at A and extend ribbon to B. Pierce center of ribbon at B, giving ribbon a little slack (about $1/16$"). Gently pull ribbon through to back of fabric and the stitch will curl at the tip as ribbon is pulled gently. Do not pull ribbon too tightly or curl will disappear.

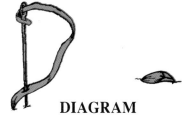

DIAGRAM

Rosette

Cut 7-mm silk ribbon 9" long; cut 4-mm silk ribbon 5" long. Adjust different widths of ribbon accordingly. Make a center post for rose bud. Fold ribbon diagonally to back. Wrap center around center post and stitch. Fold ribbon to back. Wrap. Repeat for half of length of ribbon. Gather stitch along bottom edge of remaining ribbon. Taper stitches across end. Pull thread to gather. Position ruffle around folded center and secure with stitches.

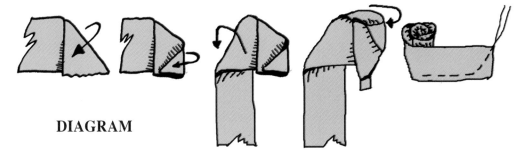

DIAGRAM

118

119

Letter

Place six strands of green embroidery floss on fabric, forming a stem in the shape of the letter "S". COUCH to secure.

Sunflower

1. Using dark yellow 4-mm silk ribbon, stitch twelve BULLIONED LAZY DAISY STITCHES; see diagram.

2. Using medium yellow 4-mm silk ribbon, stitch BULLIONED LAZY DAISY STITCHES placed slightly inward and between previous row; see diagram.

3. Using light yellow 4-mm silk ribbon, stitch ONE-TWIST RIBBON STITCHES slightly inward from BULLIONED LAZY DAISY STITCHES. Using two shades of gold 4-mm silk ribbon, fill inner circle with FRENCH KNOTS; see diagram.

Step 1   **Step 2**   **Step 3**

DIAGRAM

4. To make stems, tape a 12" length of green embroidery floss to work surface. Hold the end of the length of floss and twist it so that it becomes completely and tightly coiled. Place your finger in the center of the coiled floss; then fold the end up to meet the taped end. The floss will magically double-coil itself. Tie a knot at the cut ends to hold the coiling in place; see diagram. Repeat to make a second stem. Stitch stems to fabric with one strand of floss.

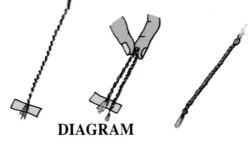

DIAGRAM

5. Thread a large needle with green ¼" satin ribbon. Bring the needle up through the fabric, folding the ribbon into a point. Then bring the needle down through the fabric, forming a pointed leaf; see diagram. Tack the point of the leaf to fabric with thread to secure. Repeat to make four leaves.

DIAGRAM

Sweet Peas

There are six different colors of sweet peas. Each sweet pea is made up of three shades of a color. Stitch variations of sweet peas by using assorted colors and sizes of silk ribbon.

1. To make buds, use 7-mm silk ribbon and stitch LAZY DAISY STITCHES.

2. To make half blooms, use 7-mm silk ribbon and STITCH LAZY DAISY STITCHES, forming center. Using 4-mm silk ribbon, stitch a SELF SELVAGE GATHERED STITCH that cups around the base of the LAZY DAISY STITCH; see diagram.

3. For a full bloom, make a half bloom, and then use a different shade of 4-mm silk ribbon and stitch another SELF SELVAGE GATHERED STITCH around the previous one; see diagram.

4. Using green 4-mm silk ribbon, stitch STRAIGHT STITCHES around the base of the flowers; see diagram. Stitch small RIBBON STITCHES into the buds; see diagram.

  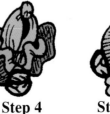

Step 2 **Step 3** **Step 4** **Step 5**

DIAGRAM

5. Using one strand of embroidery floss, COUCH tendrils of the sweet pea vine.

6. Using 4-mm silk ribbon, stitch RIBBON STITCHES and ONE-TWIST RIBBON STITCHES, forming leaves.

Strawberries

1. Place six strands of embroidery floss on fabric, forming vines. COUCH to secure.

2. Using three shades of green 4-mm silk ribbon, stitch a BULLION LAZY DAISY STITCH with a RIBBON STITCH extending from the bottom to one side of the LAZY DAISY STITCH, forming leaves.

3. Using red 4-mm silk ribbon, stitch LAZY DAISY STITCHES, forming strawberries. Using one strand of brown embroidery floss, stitch STRAIGHT STITCHES on strawberry, forming seeds.

Self Selvage Gathered Ribbon Stitch

1. Knot one end of 4-mm silk ribbon. Bring ribbon up at A; see diagram. With a needle, separate a strong thread from the selvage of the ribbon; see diagram.

2. Pull the thread to gather ribbon to desired length.

3. Bring the ribbon down through the fabric at B; see diagram. Secure ribbon to wrong side of stitching.

A

B

DIAGRAM

Squared-Off Petal

A squared-off petal will flare rather than cup, providing the length of the interval is greater than the width of the ribbon. Mark ribbon according to specific instructions. Stitch a GATHERING STITCH along markings. Pull ribbon to gather; secure thread. Shape. Stitch to fabric.

DIAGRAM

Straight Stitch

Bring needle to top of fabric at A. Insert needle into fabric at B. Straighten ribbon over finger to remove any twists. Gently pull ribbon through to the underside of the fabric.

DIAGRAM

Stem Stitch

Work from left to right to make slightly slanting stitches along the line of the stem. Bring thread up at A and insert needle under fabric at B. Bring needle up at C (halfway between A and B). Make all stitches the same length. Insert needle under fabric at D (half the length of the stitch beyond B). Bring needle up at end of previous stitch. End by taking needle to back at E.

DIAGRAM

A C B D E

Spider Mum

For each spider mum, alternately use three shades of red 4-mm silk ribbon.

1. Stitch the center of the spider mum with a BULLIONED LAZY DAISY STITCH. Stitch three TWISTED RIBBON STITCHES; see diagram.

2. Continue to fill area with TWISTED RIBBON STITCHES; see diagram.

Step 1

Step 2

Step 3

DIAGRAM

3. Stitch LOOPED RIBBON STITCHES in a cluster with the darkest shade of ribbon. Using two shades of green 4-mm silk ribbon, stitch a combination of leaves using the BULLIONED LAZY DAISY STITCH and the RIBBON STITCH.

Satin-Style Stitch

Satin-style stitches offer a smooth, shiny surface that creates a change of texture. To create this effect, place stitches side by side, so that the underlying fabric does not show through.

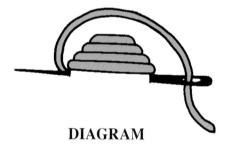

DIAGRAM

Stylized Columbine

1. Using light pink ³/₈" organza ribbon, stitch BULLIONED LAZY DAISY STITCHES, forming the tops of the flowers; see diagram. Stitch RIBBON STITCHES between BULLIONED LAZY DAISY STITCHES; see diagram.

DIAGRAM

2. Using rose 4-mm silk ribbon, stitch long ONE-TWIST RIBBON STITCHES to form the bottoms of the flowers; see diagram.

3. Using pink ³/₈" organza ribbon, stitch RIBBON STITCHES at the middle of each flower; see diagram.

4. Using one strand of yellow embroidery floss, stitch PISTIL STITCHES at center of each flower; see diagram.

Step 2

Step 3

Step 4

DIAGRAM

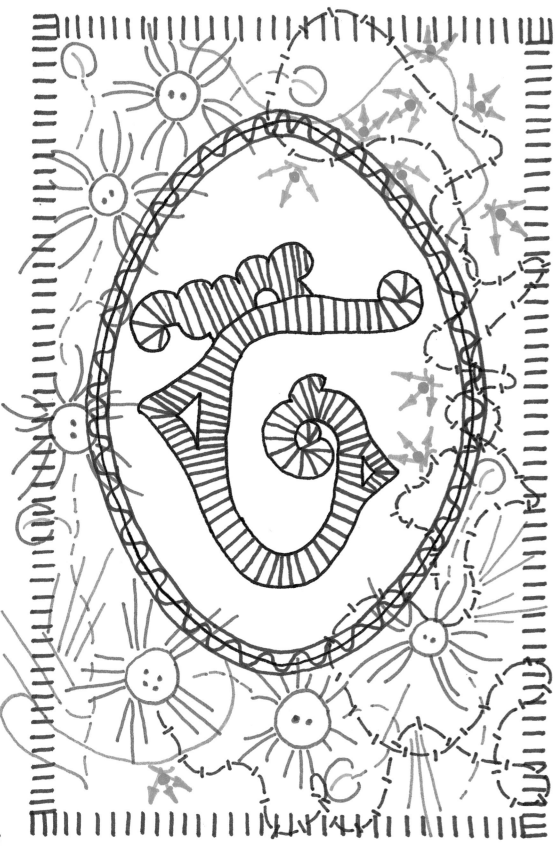

T

Letter

1. Using 4-mm silk ribbon, stitch STRAIGHT STITCHES, SATIN-STITCH STYLE, to form the letter "T". Outline the letter with embroidery floss, using STRAIGHT STITCHES.

2. Using 4-mm silk ribbon, stitch STRAIGHT STITCHES to form border.

3. Using 7-mm silk ribbon, make MJ'S FLUTING; see photo. Using embroidery floss, stitch STRAIGHT STITCHES on center of fluting; see photo.

Thumbagaria

1. Using embroidery floss, stitch RUNNING STITCHES, forming vines.

2. Weave 7-mm silk ribbon through RUNNING STITCHES; see diagram.

DIAGRAM

3. Using one shade of 7-mm silk ribbon, stitch a LAZY DAISY STITCH at ends of vines to form buds. Using a second shade of 7-mm silk ribbon, stitch a STRAIGHT STITCH in center of LAZY DAISY STITCH.

Tiger Lily

1. Using 13-mm silk ribbon, stitch large STRAIGHT STITCHES, forming leaves. PAD stitches by layering them on top of one another.

2. Repeat Step 1, stitching flower petals.

3. Stitch buttons at centers of flowers.

Trumpet Vine

1. Using embroidery floss, stitch BACKSTITCHES, then whip-stitch around them, forming, vines.

2. Place braided trim on fabric, forming vines; tack with invisible stitches.

3. Using 4-mm silk ribbon, stitch three RIBBON STITCHES with a FRENCH KNOT at the center. Stitch a STRAIGHT STITCH at base, forming calyx.

Twisted Ribbon Stitch

Bring needle up at A. Extend ribbon its full length and twirl needle so that ribbon coils, but not so tight that it buckles. Insert needle back into twisted ribbon at desired stitch length. Pull ribbon through to wrong side of fabric, allowing some of the bunched ribbon to remain on the surface.

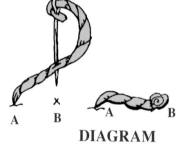

DIAGRAM

132

Letter

1. Coil dark gold embroidery floss together; see directions for Sunflower on page 120. Place coiled floss on fabric, forming the outline of the letter "U". COUCH to secure. Coil light gold embroidery floss and fill outline.

2. Weave dark purple 4-mm silk ribbon through the right edges of the outlined letter.

Umbelliferea (Dill Flowers)

1. Using five shades of gold 4-mm silk ribbon, stitch FRENCH KNOTS.

2. Tack bright gold and bronze seed beads to each cluster of FRENCH KNOTS.

3. Place green rattail on fabric, forming stems. COUCH to secure. Using three strands of green embroidery floss, stitch STEM STITCHES for the narrow stems and STRAIGHT STITCHES for the leaves.

Astrautia Flowers

See Astrautia Flowers on page 17.

Eryingium

See Eryingium on page 42.

136

137

Letter

1. Using green embroidery floss and three shades of rose embroidery floss, make several 8" lengths of coiled floss; see Sunflower on page 120. Shape the floss to form the letter "V". Secure with invisible stitches. Stitch seed beads as desired.

2. Make three rosettes; see Rosettes on page 116. Stitch rosettes on the letter "V". Stitch leaves with STRAIGHT STITCHES and LAZY DAISY STITCHES. Stitch rose buds with BULLIONED LAZY DAISY STITCHES.

Violets

1. Cut a 7³/₈" length of ⁵/₈" purple iridescent wired ribbon. Beginning and ending ¹/₄" from ends, mark ribbon at 1³/₈" intervals; see diagram. Stitch a GATHERING STITCH along blue stitching line. Pull thread tightly to gather. Stitch first and last petals together. Repeat to make seven flowers.

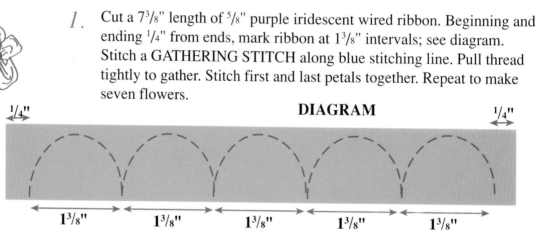

DIAGRAM

¹/₄"   ¹/₄"

1³/₈"   1³/₈"   1³/₈"   1³/₈"   1³/₈"

2. Cut three 3¹/₄" lengths and one 4⁵/₈" length of ⁵/₈" purple iridescent wired ribbon. Repeat as above, forming violet buds.

3. Cut a 5" length of 1" wired ribbon. Stitch a GATHERING STITCH along black stitching line. Pull thread tightly to gather, forming leaf; see diagram. Repeat to make three leaves.

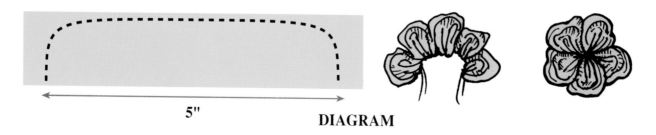

5"

DIAGRAM

4. Using green 4-mm silk ribbon, stitch STRAIGHT STITCHES at bases of the buds. Stitch RIBBON STITCHES onto the body of the buds, forming the calyx.

5. Using four green shades of embroidery floss, make twelve 4$\frac{1}{2}$" lengths of coiled floss; see Sunflower on page 120. Stitch each length at top and bottom only, forming stems.

6. Cut a 15" length of $\frac{1}{2}$" satin ribbon, and tie a bow. Stitch to fabric below violet bunch.

Pansies
See Pansies on page 100.

Johnny Jump-Ups
See Johnny Jump-Ups on page 68.

141

Letter

1. Using gold silk embroidery floss, stitch STRAIGHT STITCHES, SATIN-STITCH STYLE, forming the letter "W".

2. Using four shades of gray 4-mm silk ribbon, stitch LAZY DAISY STITCHES, forming small flowers. Using green 4-mm silk ribbon, stitch RIBBON STITCHES, forming leaves. Stitch seed beads where desired.

Wisteria

1. Cut twenty-four 3" lengths of 2¼" silk organza fabric. Fold fabric in half lengthwise; press.

2. Fold ribbon as shown in diagram and secure with stitches.

3. Stitch a GATHERING STITCH along remaining length of ribbon.

4. Pull thread tightly to gather; secure thread.

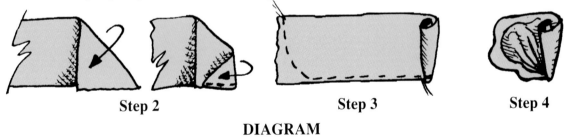

Step 2   **Step 3**   **Step 4**

DIAGRAM

5. Cut twenty 2" lengths from 2 ¼" silk organdy. Stitch and fold each length as in Steps 1–4.

6. Place several petals in place and hold with pins. Hand-stitch gathered edge to fabric. Using ivory 7-mm silk ribbon, cover gathered edge with two STRAIGHT STITCHES. Continue to place and stitch petals and leaves until all are stitched to the fabric.

7. Tack antique pearls where desired.

Wisteria Leaves

1. Cut five 5" lengths of light green ⅝" wired ribbon. Stitch GATHER-ING STITCHES, as shown in Diagram. Pull tightly to gather. Shape leaf.

2. Repeat Step 1 using five 5" lengths of dark green ⅝" wired ribbon.

DIAGRAM

146

Letter

1. To make vase, place ³/₄" metallic lace edge to edge; cut to fit shape and hand-stitch in place. Outline vase with metallic braid to cover raw edges of lace.

2. Handling three strands of metallic cord as one, form the letter "X" on vase. COUCH to secure. Repeat to make handle of vase. Weave an additional layer of metallic cord through the handle and the letter "X" on vase.

3. Tie a bow with two shades of 7-mm silk ribbon. Stitch in place. CASCADE the tails.

Lilacs

See Lilacs on page 80.

Gardenia

See Gardenia on page 52.

Morning Glories

See Morning Glories on page 86.

Stylized Columbine

See Stylized Columbine on page 125.

Peonies

See Peonies on page 102.

Heather

See Heather on page 57.

Letter

1. Using dark gray 4-mm silk ribbon, stitch RIBBON STITCHES, SATIN-STITCH STYLE, forming the letter "Y".

2. Place antique cotton lace on fabric, forming a box border; secure with small stitches. Make a bow with ⅝" satin and wired ribbon. Tack to fabric. Stitch buttons where desired.

Yarrow Clusters

1. Using four shades of yellow 4-mm silk ribbon, stitch FRENCH KNOTS in clusters, randomly alternating shades.

2. Using green embroidery floss, stitch STEM STITCHES to form stems. Stitch STRAIGHT STITCHES around stems, forming leaves.

154

Letter

1. Using one shade of 4-mm silk ribbon, stitch a RUNNING STITCH, forming border. Weave a second shade of 4-mm silk ribbon around RUNNING STITCHES; see diagram.

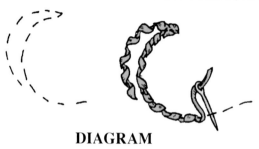

DIAGRAM

2. Using 4-mm silk ribbon, stitch STRAIGHT STITCHES, SATIN-STITCH STYLE, to form the letter "Z". Using embroidery floss, stitch a BACKSTITCH through center of letter.

3. Using 4-mm silk ribbon, outline letter with a BACKSTITCH.

4. Using 4-mm silk ribbon, stitch LAZY DAISY STITCHES TO form oval around letter.

5. Using 4-mm silk ribbon, stitch FRENCH KNOTS between LAZY DAISY STITCHES.

6. Repeat Step 1 on inside edge of oval and to form inner border.

Zinnia Leaves and Stems

1. Cut a 1¹/₂" length of ⁵/₈" wired ribbon. Pinch ends together, forming points; fold pointed ends to back. Tack edges to fabric with invisible stitches. Place and shape leaves as desired or see photo.

2. Using 4-mm silk ribbon, stitch a RUNNING STITCH to form inner border. Weave ribbon through RUNNING STITCHES, forming stems; see diagram. Stitch LAZY DAISY STITCHES around stems, forming leaves.

DIAGRAM

3. Using 4-mm silk ribbon, stitch RUNNING STITCHES to form stems; place as desired.

4. Using embroidery floss, stitch FERN STITCHES; place as desired.

Zinnias

1. Using 7-mm silk ribbon, stitch LOOPED RIBBON STITCHES to form flower petals; see diagram.

2. Using 4-mm silk ribbon, stitch FRENCH KNOTS at centers of flowers; see diagram.

METRIC EQUIVALENCE CHART

MM-Millimetres   CM-Centimetres
INCHES TO MILLIMETRES AND CENTIMETRES

INCHES	MM	CM	INCHES	CM	INCHES	CM
1/8	3	0.9	9	22.9	30	76.2
1/4	6	0.6	10	25.4	31	78.7
3/8	10	1.0	11	27.9	32	81.3
1/2	13	1.3	12	30.5	33	83.8
5/8	16	1.6	13	33.0	34	86.4
3/4	19	1.9	14	35.6	35	88.9
7/8	22	2.2	15	38.1	36	91.4
1	25	2.5	16	40.6	37	94.0
1 1/4	32	3.2	17	43.2	38	96.5
1 1/2	38	3.8	18	45.7	39	99.1
1 3/4	44	4.4	19	48.3	40	101.6
2	51	5.1	20	50.8	41	104.1
2 1/2	64	6.4	21	53.3	42	106.7
3	76	7.6	22	55.9	43	109.2
3 1/2	89	8.9	23	58.4	44	111.8
4	102	10.2	24	61.0	45	114.3
4 1/2	114	11.4	25	63.5	46	116.8
5	127	12.7	26	66.0	47	119.4
6	152	15.2	27	68.6	48	121.9
7	178	17.8	28	71.1	49	124.5
8	203	20.3	29	73.7	50	127.0

YARDS TO METRES

YARDS	METRES	YARDS	METRES	YARDS	METRES	YARDS	METRES	YARDS	METRES
1/8	0.11	2 1/8	1.94	4 1/8	3.77	6 1/8	5.60	8 1/8	7.43
1/4	0.23	2 1/4	2.06	4 1/4	3.89	6 1/4	5.72	8 1/4	7.54
3/8	0.34	2 3/8	2.17	4 3/8	4.00	6 3/8	5.83	8 3/8	7.66
1/2	0.46	2 1/2	2.29	4 1/2	4.11	6 1/2	5.94	8 1/2	7.77
5/8	0.57	2 5/8	2.40	4 5/8	4.23	6 5/8	6.06	8 5/8	7.89
3/4	0.69	2 3/4	2.51	4 3/4	4.34	6 3/4	6.17	8 3/4	8.00
7/8	0.80	2 7/8	2.63	4 7/8	4.46	6 7/8	6.29	8 7/8	8.12
1	0.91	3	2.74	5	4.57	7	6.40	9	8.23
1 1/8	1.03	3 1/8	2.86	5 1/8	4.69	7 1/8	6.52	9 1/8	8.34
1 1/4	1.14	3 1/4	2.97	5 1/4	4.80	7 1/4	6.63	9 1/4	8.46
1 3/8	1.26	3 3/8	3.09	5 3/8	4.91	7 3/8	6.74	9 3/8	8.57
1 1/2	1.37	3 1/2	3.20	5 1/2	5.03	7 1/2	6.86	9 1/2	8.69
1 5/8	1.49	3 5/8	3.31	5 5/8	5.14	7 5/8	6.97	9 5/8	8.80
1 3/4	1.60	3 3/4	3.43	5 3/4	5.26	7 3/4	7.09	9 3/4	8.92
1 7/8	1.71	3 7/8	3.54	5 7/8	5.37	7 7/8	7.20	9 7/8	9.03
2	1.83	4	3.66	6	5.49	8	7.32	10	9.14

Index